God Will Make A Way

Amazing Affirmations of
God's Faithfulness
in Everyday Life

Thelma Wells

OLIVER
NELSON

THOMAS NELSON PUBLISHERS
Nashville

Published in Nashville, Tennessee, by Thomas Nelson, Inc.

Scripture quotations noted NKJV are from THE NEW KING JAMES VERSION. Copyright © 1979, 1980, 1982, Thomas Nelson, Inc., Publishers.

Scripture quotations noted NIV are from the HOLY BIBLE: NEW INTERNATIONAL VERSION®. Copyright © 1973, 1978, 1984 by International Bible Society. Used by permission of Zondervan Publishing House. All rights reserved.

Scripture quotations noted NASB are from the NEW AMERICAN STANDARD BIBLE ®. © Copyright The Lockman Foundation 1960, 1962, 1963, 1968, 1971, 1972, 1973, 1975, 1977. Used by permission.

Scripture quotations noted KJV are from THE KING JAMES VERSION of the Bible.

Library of Congress Cataloging-in-Publication Data

Wells, Thelma, 1941–
    God will make a way : amazing affirmations of God's faithfulness in everyday life / Thelma Wells.
      p.   cm.
    Includes bibliographical references.
    ISBN 0-7852-7542-8 (hardcover)
    1. God—Promises—Meditations. I. Title.
BT180.P7W45 1998
231.7—dc21   97–52366
                                          CIP

Printed in the United States of America.

1 2 3 4 5 6 QPK 03 02 01 00 99 98

In memory of Granny Sarah Harrell,

my sainted great-grandmother,

and Lawrence Morris Sr., my grandfather,

the two people who played the most significant roles

in developing my character and values.

Praise be to the LORD,

who has given rest to his people Israel just as he promised.

Not one word has failed of all the good promises

he gave through his servant Moses.

(1 Kings 8:56 NIV)

Contents

Acknowledgments

To Vikki Lynn Wells, my first daughter: She knows me better than most people. She has seen me trust God to make a way and then experience His provision through financial troubles, heartache, disappointment, sickness, loss of loved ones, career changes, relationship issues, academic pursuits, and other uncertainties. She rejoiced with me when I was happy, excited, pleasantly surprised; when I received awards and excelled in accomplishments; and in many other wonderful times in my life. She was a midwife to the birth of these stories I am now privileged to share with you, the reader. It was her creative expertise, compassionate prodding, and faith in a publisher's vision for the merit of such a book that sparked the fire of its development.

Vikki, if it were not for you, this idea would still be a daydream instead of a dream come true. Thank you!

To my husband: You're my greatest Hollywood agent, my divine-right mate. Thank God for you!

To my son, George, and daughter Lesa: God blessed me when He made you my children. You bring me happiness and make me proud to be your mother.

To all of the magnificent people mentioned in this book: God has put me in contact with you. I am grateful to you for these life experiences.

To Rolf Zettersten and Victor Oliver: You believed in me. I appreciate you!

To Traci Mullins and Kathryn A. Yanni: One of the most fantastic writers/editors in the world and the most fantastic literary agent in the world. Thank you, ladies!

Introduction

God
Will Make
a Way

"The Lord will make a way somehow." Granny's faith-filled words still ring in my ears. Granny taught me that God is the God of the morning, noonday, afternoon, evening, and midnight hour. God is the ruler of the planets, sun, moon, stars, atoms, space, time, energy, gravity, formulas, hypotheses, birth, breath, life, and death. He controls our going out and our coming in. He blesses our sitting down and our standing up. He carves our names in the palms of His hands, and if we let Him, He intimately directs our steps. The circumstances of our lives are no secret to Him, for He knows our innermost thoughts and desires. He knows far better than we do exactly what we need, and He has promised to meet us at every turn to show us we are precious to Him. His Word is overflowing with promises of His faithfulness to us.

Biblical scholars say that there are more than 37,000 promises in the Word of God—promises to comfort us, love us, prosper us, forgive us, protect us, bless us, prepare us, reward us, and on and on. A promise is a pledge, covenant, or contract to another to fulfill a specific action. Granny always seemed so sure that God would fulfill His promises, and I wanted to grow in the kind of faith that she had. I began studying God's promises out of curiosity. I started wondering what I could expect from God. What had He pledged to me personally? Although I knew He had made promises to Abraham regarding his offspring, to Moses and the people of Israel, to the disciples, and to future believers, I wondered how those promises related to me today.

As I began studying, I found myself reminiscing and reflecting. When I read, "He shall give His angels charge over you, / To keep you in all your ways" (Ps. 91:11 NKJV), I remembered the time my car slid across the highway and crashed. Amazingly I emerged without a scratch. When I read, "God will meet all your needs according to his glorious riches in Christ Jesus" (Phil. 4:19 NIV), I recalled the time I really needed $26,000 in three weeks, and God supplied my need. When I read, "Train up a child in the way he should go, / And when he is old he will not depart from it"

(Prov. 22:6 NKJV), I thought about children who were addicted to drugs throughout their youth but today are living productive lives.

I got excited! I was on to something. In my fifty-six years of living, God's promises had been fulfilled over and over again in my daily life. I could no longer view ordinary situations—life's ups and downs—as mere coincidences. Now I could see them clearly: as the real-life unfolding of God's promises to me. My God was a God of His Word, and my life was packed with evidence of His faithfulness.

When I was a child, He rescued me and saved me. When I was a teenager, He renewed Himself in me and gave me peace and comfort. When I became an adult, He delivered me from self-destruction. Since I've become a mature adult, He has healed my body and delivered my children and opened doors I needed to walk through while closing doors that were not in His plan for me. God, through His Son, Jesus, has put a song in my heart and praise on my lips. He has taken the broken pieces of my life and restored them to me more perfectly than before they were broken. And He wants to do the same things for you. He longs to show Himself faithful to His creation.

When you walk with Him, He will reveal to you who you are in Him and what He has for you to do. He has given you His Word so that you will know His thoughts toward you and His plans for you. When you hide His Word in your heart, you will have joy unspeakable as you discover that He keeps His word to you always.

What a mighty, tender, and awesome God we serve! That's why angels bow before Him and heaven and earth adore Him. And so do I, because He has shown me His faithfulness. In this book I have recorded some of my experiences that have confirmed to me God's commitment to fulfill His Word in my life. Each story is personal and true, and each promise fulfilled is a snapshot of the character of God. If God fulfills His promises in my life, then He is doing the same in yours because He has given each of us His Word. As you read about the moments in my life that have transformed my understanding of God, I pray you will recognize and recall similar moments from your history. We all have them if we open our eyes to see.

I believe that God's promises bring great hope. As I have embraced and personally celebrated God's promises to me, I have felt completely reborn. Liberated. Overjoyed. May you find this same hope and joy as you discover that your Father in heaven is indeed a God of His Word. God will make a way!

> *For the LORD is good and his love endures forever;*
> *his faithfulness continues through all generations.*
>   *(Ps. 100:5 NIV)*

Bee Your Best!

God
Promises to
Encourage Us

⚛

$\mathcal{J}$ust about everyone who is acquainted with me knows I wear a bumblebee brooch every day. People have heard me make reference to the bumblebee in many of my speeches. This is by design. My motto, "In Christ, you can be the best of what you want to BEE!" has encouraged me through the thick and thin of my life.

I realize the bumblebee has no power of its own to make me be my best. Some people even think it's trite. But I am amazed that the bee is able to do what God designed it to do in spite of its scientific limitations. You see, the body of a bumblebee is too big, its wingspan too narrow, for it to be able to fly. Yet it flies around anyway doing what God made it to do. It defies the laws of nature but adheres to the law of God!

Human beings need a lot of encouragement to be able to do the things required and desired of them. Sometimes I've gotten bogged down in the pity parties of life, and I've tried to deny that I have the ability to do whatever God wants me to. But I know He doesn't assign me anything I can't handle.

Sometimes I have to take inventory of who I am in Him by asking myself:

- Who am I?
- What is my mission?
- What is my vision?
- What is my passion?
- Where do I want to be at this stage in my life?
- How do I know I can accomplish all these things?

These are some of the answers I get when I talk to myself:

Who Am I?

I am a child of God with God-given talent, skill, and ability. I know that "I can do all things through Christ who strengthens me" (Phil. 4:13 NKJV).

I understand that I have intellect and common sense, but that I'm not smart enough to outthink, outgive, and outdo God.

I realize that even though I do some things well, I am not a master of all trades. Therefore, I recognize my limitations. When tasks come along that I don't do well or don't need to do myself, I delegate them, hire them out, or get rid of them.

- I am a wonderful wife, a beloved mother, and a proud grandmother.
- I enjoy making people happy.
- I am a speaker, author, singer, and businesswoman.
- I enjoy studying the Bible, going to church socials, watching Christian television, and traveling.
- I enjoy learning and staying ahead of the game.
- I am a risk taker and adventurer.
- I am a true friend.
- I am attractive and enjoy dressing attractively.
- My daughter Lesa calls me a Proverbs 31 woman.

What Is My Mission?

My mission is to travel globally, extracting diamonds out of people's dust. I believe that all people have so much good in them—talent, skill, life experiences that can help them live an abundant life through Jesus Christ. I believe my mission is to take people a message of hope, inspiration, and encouragement to motivate them to look deep inside themselves and realize their potential as well as extract the strengths that can help them achieve their purpose in life. All of us are as frail as dust, but when given the opportunity to achieve and excel, we become stronger with each success.

What Is My Vision?

I see myself traveling around the world, talking to huge audiences about the restoring power of God.

I see my books appearing in every possible location in the world.

I see people accepting Christ as a result of hearing me speak and reading my books.

What Is My Passion?

My passion is delivering the Word of God.

Where Do I Want to Be at This Stage in My Life?

I want to be in the perfect will of God in my business, family, church, civic, leisure, academic, relational, and all other pursuits.

This is a lofty desire because sometimes I don't know God's will for my life. However, within the past five years I have used a method that seems to work for me. Before I become involved in a business venture, speak, join a committee, go on vacation, or deal with a difficult relationship, I go to the Word of God to see what the Bible might have to say about the situation. Then I pray for wisdom and guidance. I know God is a God of order, and I depend on Him to bring order into whatever I'm contemplating. If I run into a lot of problems and things just don't seem to be working out, and if the outer chaos is matched by an inner disease about my involvement, then I take it as my sign that I'm outside the perfect will of God. I have found that God communicates with each of us in ways we can understand, and I know I can count on Him to direct me clearly in whatever He has for me to do.

How Do I Know I Can Accomplish All These Things?

I know I can accomplish all these things because God doesn't give me a passion or direction that cannot be accomplished in one way or another. I may not see the finished product, but He will let me see the beginning and let me know that He has someone in place to carry it farther.

The exercise I've just done is an example of what you can do to find out what you want to be when you "grow up." Maybe you already know what you want to be. Maybe you're being what you want to be. But I've discovered that when people get what they want, they usually want more or something different. To BEE my best, I must stay in contact with God and with myself. I must never get so busy that I have prolonged out-of-mind experiences that keep me from being in touch with God's will and my own best interests.

If you want to be your best, encourage other people. Compliment them. Do something nice for them without expecting anything in return. Pray. Read your Bible. Read good books. Go to church. Enjoy fun activities. Watch what you eat. Take a vacation. Relax. Smell the roses. Seek God! Continue doing whatever keeps you in touch with God. He knows the plans He has for you and the ways He will accomplish them through you.

PRAYER

Wonderful Master, You give me the opportunity to be my best. You've been the example of what is the best. Your guidelines for daily living set the stage and create the finale of what is best in Your sight. When I take inventory of myself, You are right there with me, evaluating the ways I live, seeing if I am obedient to Your course for my life. The way is narrow but straight. If I stay on the path You direct, I will have few delays and no fatalities. Thank You for Your encouragement. Thank You that You had me and Your plans for me already established before the world began. If I am ever out of line with Your mission, vision, and passion for me, quickly let me know. Amen.

GOD'S WORD TO YOU

"For I know the plans I have for you," declares the LORD, "plans to prosper you and not to harm you, plans to give you hope and a future." (Jer. 29:11 NIV)

AFFIRMATION

In Christ, I can be the best of what I want to be.

Angels Watching Over Me

God Promises
Ministering Angels

There is an angel craze these days. People—I am one of them—are collecting angel paraphernalia (books, pictures, ceramics, lamps, jewelry, greeting cards, and all sorts of things). But I wonder if people realize the significance of real angels.

One rainy October day, a woman with whom I had met to discuss a business plan called me when she returned to her office in another state. We talked about the torrential rain, and she told me what happened when she'd stopped for gas on her way home from the airport. At the service station, the attendant discovered that she had a flat tire. "God sure knows how to protect us," she commented. "Just think what could have happened if I'd gotten on the freeway and had a blowout in this rain." I believe angels were protecting her.

That same night as I was heading home from the television station on the rain-slick road, my car hydroplaned and glided uncontrollably from the center lane into the extreme left-hand lane. I was on a freeway that was ordinarily crowded but at that moment had absolutely no oncoming traffic. I believe angels were protecting me.

Several years ago, the roads were icy as I traveled to Fort Worth from Dallas on Interstate 30. Just over the Oakland Street exit, I hit an icy patch that caused my car to slide from the right-hand lane over four lanes into the median. *Crash! Bang!* I was stuck in the ditch with wheels spinning, the hood and side bent. Amazingly I was not frightened. I rocked the car back and forth between first gear and reverse and managed to get it out of the ditch and back on the freeway. The car slid toward the opposite side of the freeway. Cars were coming. But I was calmly praying. I saw the oncoming cars literally freeze in place and time as my car, without significant help from me, placed itself in the correct lane headed in the correct direction toward Fort Worth. The peace I felt made it seem as if nothing had happened, and there were absolutely no cars coming toward me. I felt totally safe. Something stopped the cars. Time stopped for me. It's still amazing as I picture that scene in my mind today. I knew then and am still convinced that ministering angels held those oncoming cars in place, straightened my car, and pointed me in the right direction.

Maybe you haven't experienced anything that dramatic. Or maybe you've had similar experiences and just thought they were coincidences. In my opinion, there are no coincidences. When we make Jesus Christ the Lord of our lives, the Lord orders everything that happens to us. Psalm 37:23–24 says that when the Lord approves of a person's path, He makes that person's steps firm; even if the person stumbles, he won't fall because the Lord upholds him.

In the back pages of the Ryrie Study Bible, there is a complete study on the doctrine of angels. I've spent a lot of time in this study getting to know more and more about what angels are; how many there are; what form they have; what works they do; how God uses them on behalf of the believer, the church, the nation, and the world; and how they can work in the lives of sinners.

I have heard many stories from Christians about their experiences with angels. Ruth Cummings has a powerful story. Ruth had been to a workshop where I was teaching about angels. She had given very little thought about angels working in her life, but after hearing about what Scripture had to say about them, she decided to test what she had learned.

Ruth and her husband, Tony, had been trying to conceive a child for nearly ten years with no success. They had spent thousands of dollars on fertility processes, to no avail. They had given up on those processes. But in her soul, Ruth believed that God had a baby in His plans for their family.

Ruth was riding in her car one day and started talking to God, asking Him to dispatch His ministering angels to get her baby. One month later she conceived, and today Ruth and Tony have a handsome son. Ruth knows God allowed His angels to work in their lives.

If you are unsure about the work that angels do in your life, study the Word of God about them. Read books about angels. I believe it is imperative that we compare what any author says with the truth of the holy Scriptures, but Christians have written many good books about angels. Dr. Billy Graham's *Angels: God's Secret Agents* is one of the easiest to read and understand. Edward P. Myers's *A Study of Angels Systematic Bible Doctrines* is also good.

I enjoy singing this Negro spiritual:

All night, All day, Angels watching over me, my Lord,
All night, All day, Angels watching over me.
Now I lay me down to sleep.
Angels watching over me, my Lord.
Pray the Lord my soul to keep.
Angels watching over me.

It's such a comfort to know that wherever we are, wherever we go, God has ministering angels available to assist us.

PRAYER

Knowing that Your ministering angels protect Your children gives me security as I travel through dangers seen and unseen. I appreciate how You reveal Your truths to us through circumstances and situations that we cannot adequately explain. We know in our hearts that You are using these situations to confirm truths to us. You have confirmed in many situations that angels work on our behalf, doing Your perfect will in our lives as well as in the universe. Thank You for dispatching Your angels to protect and guide Your children. Amen.

GOD'S WORD TO YOU

For he will command his angels concerning you
   to guard you in all your ways;
they will lift you up in their hands,
   so that you will not strike your foot against a stone.
You will tread upon the lion and the cobra;
   you will trample the great lion and the serpent.
   (Ps. 91:11–13 NIV)

GOD WILL MAKE A WAY

AFFIRMATION

I am confident that angels work to carry out God's
will in my life.

No Respecter of Persons

God Promises to Love Without Bias

*E*arly one fall morning I was walking out of the Earle Cabbell Federal Building in downtown Dallas after teaching a course for the Federal Credit Union. That particular morning I was dressed in my corporate attire and had my attaché case in hand that bespoke of my being a powerful corporate executive.

Walking toward me was a woman who looked tired, dirty, unkempt, and smelly. She approached me and asked, "Lady, would you give me a quarter?" I responded to her in a way I am not proud of. Rude, arrogant, haughty, and judgmental summed up my attitude toward her. With an alienating voice and an unfriendly look, I exclaimed to her, "I don't have a quarter!" Then I turned to walk away.

At the very moment when I turned to walk away, the Holy Spirit convicted me. I turned back toward the woman and asked her why she needed a quarter. "I need to catch the bus," she replied. I told her that I had lied, then pulled out my change purse and emptied it into her hand. She ran and caught the bus.

I crossed the street to the lot where my car was parked and slumped into my seat in tears. I was appalled at myself. *How could I have been so rude and insensitive to that woman?* Sure, she was dirty, disheveled, and begging, but I didn't know her circumstances. Even if I hadn't wanted to give her a quarter, I could have been respectful of her as a human being.

I was shocked to discover that I was prejudiced—prejudiced against people because of the way they look! I'm ashamed to admit that when I first saw that woman, only three things came to mind: drugs, alcohol, *get a job*. Yet I knew nothing about her. My perception of her caused me to be so rude. I assumed something without having any facts.

As I sat in the car I thought, *That woman could have been an unemployed banker.* Banks had failed in Dallas, and some of the executives I knew had been without a job for a year or more. Or she could have been running away from somebody or something. I didn't know her circumstances, and I certainly didn't have the right to play God.

That woman did me more good than my quarter did her. She caused me to look more critically at my biases and prejudices and begin to work on myself. Where had my bigoted thoughts come from? I don't remember having any experience that caused me to feel that way.

In this multicultural world, the list of different people grows constantly. People differ in ways that don't matter to some people but cause others major discomfort.

I recently saw a talk show that featured a woman who learned firsthand that many people have deep prejudice against people they consider extremely fat. As an experiment, she had a "fat suit" made and wore it in many social and business situations. During some of those occasions, she was laughed at, stared at when she dined in public, and called a fat pig and other derogatory names.

I remember reading a survey that determined skin color was the thing that caused many people to push others out of their lives within the first seven seconds of seeing them. "True Colors," the title of a 1991 documentary on *20/20,* revealed the blatant prejudice shown a young black man when he and a fellow young white man went out to interview for jobs. Their secret mission was to test if there was real or only perceived prejudice among potential employers.

The documentary confirmed an overwhelming amount of prejudice against the black man. Even though he had the same set of skills and personal attributes as the white man, he was treated completely differently during the job interviews and was never hired.

Prejudice is a strong feeling for or against something without many facts to support it. It usually comes from misinformation or distorted information about another person or group of people. In a cultural diversity class I taught once, I invited people to discuss anything about their culture that they wanted others to know. In return, the other participants could ask them anything they wanted to know but had been afraid to ask. One woman didn't ask any questions. However, she was very interested in what was being said. I noticed she was almost sitting on the edge of her chair the whole time.

Shortly after the seminar, I got a heart-wrenching five-page letter from that woman. She said that all her life she had been told that black men were rapists and killers. She was warned never to be alone with one. When she moved to a big city and found out she had to work where black men worked, she was petrified. She said she would not go to the water fountain, rest room, or break room without someone to accompany her because so many black men were in the company. She could not understand why all the other white women were not afraid of them. Of course, she never told anyone why she needed an escort everywhere she went. Her coworkers assumed she liked a lot of company.

During my seminar, for the first time in her life she came to grips with the fact that she had been sold a bill of goods about black men. She said that the healing process began that day, and she was so thankful for the startling education she received from attending my class.

As followers of Christ's teachings, Christians should have no place in their lives for prejudice against any human being. The woman who didn't look and smell as I thought she should was only one step from where I could be, were it not for the grace of God. The late Dr. Ernest Coble Estell Sr. quoted this favorite saying from his pulpit at St. John Missionary Baptist Church in Dallas: "It's one step from where I am to where you have to go." When I was a little girl, that saying didn't mean a thing to me, but now I understand it.

When Christ went to Calvary, I am so glad He had absolutely no prejudices or biases. He was no respecter of persons; He died for us all. If God were prejudiced, I might have been relegated to the you-can't-make-it-to-heaven group. I was poor and fat once, and I'll be black all my life. Praise God, none of that matters. The *only* things that matter are my love for God and my faith in His Son, Jesus Christ.

PRAYER

Jesus, You set the pattern for my relationships with "other" people—people who don't look like me, talk like me, live like me. When You called Your disciples, You selected individuals whom most people would have overlooked because of their profession or social status. You chose to visit the homes of tax collectors, crooks, and outcasts. You offered Yourself to everyone by saying, "Whosoever will, let him come to Me." Thank You, God! When people look down on me, exclude me, or don't allow me my rights as a human being, I can always depend on You to love me without bias. I can also trust You to help me be better instead of bitter. Please help me to remember to treat others the way I'd like them to treat me. Amen.

GOD'S WORD TO YOU

There is neither Jew nor Greek, there is neither slave nor free, there is neither male nor female; for you are all one in Christ Jesus. (Gal. 3:28 NKJV)

GOD WILL MAKE A WAY

AFFIRMATION

God loves everybody without bias,
and He enables me to do the same.

Oh, Blessed Savior

God Promises Salvation to Those Who Receive Christ

It was pitch-dark in the sanctuary of the St. John Missionary Baptist Church in Dallas on that Easter night in 1959. I was sitting in the balcony with my teenage friends and my boyfriend, George, watching an artist tell the story of the Crucifixion by drawing images with fluorescent chalk. The congregation was spellbound, captivated by the skill of the artist, the lifelikeness of the images, and the power of the message. Sound effects and hymns enhanced the presentation, and people began to cry, moan, gasp, and wail at the torture of our Savior.

As the artist depicted the big drops of blood raining from the crown of thorns on Jesus' head and from His pierced body, something unexplainable happened to me. It looked to me as if those drops of blood were real. That was real blood flowing from my Savior's body! Jumping to my feet, I shouted, "He lives! He lives! I know He lives!" My shouts might have reminded you of how emotional some people get when their team is winning a sporting event like the Super Bowl. I could not control the emotion. I remained in that state of holy ecstasy for what seemed like a long time.

That was a glorious night in 1959—the night the Lord Jesus Christ confirmed to me that, without a doubt, He is the Savior of the world. Since that time, I have never doubted that reality. Sometimes my faith has gotten shaky, or I've doubted my role in making our relationship what it should be. But never have I questioned the saving grace of Jesus Christ.

I love to sing the words of this hymn:

There is a name I love to hear, I love to sing its worth;
It sounds like music in my ear, The sweetest name on earth.
O, how I love Jesus. O, how I love Jesus. O, how I love Jesus!
Because He first loved me.[1]

Isaiah told of His coming hundreds of years prior to His birth,

For a child will be born to us, a son will be given to us;
And the government will rest on His shoulders;
And His name will be called Wonderful Counselor,
  Mighty God,
Eternal Father, Prince of Peace. . . .
The zeal of the LORD of hosts will accomplish this.
(Isa. 9:6–7 NASB)

Luke announced His birth: "For unto you is born this day in the city of David a Saviour, which is Christ the Lord" (Luke 2:11 KJV). Timothy told of some of His works: "But is now made manifest by the appearing of our Saviour Jesus Christ, who hath abolished death, and hath brought life and immortality to light through the gospel" (2 Tim. 1:10 KJV). Titus talked of His return: "Looking for that blessed hope, and the glorious appearing of the great God and our Saviour Jesus Christ" (Titus 2:13 KJV). John exclaimed, "And we have seen and do testify that the Father sent the Son to be the Saviour of the world" (1 John 4:14 KJV). And John declared, "For God so loved the world that He gave His only begotten Son, that whoever believes in Him should not perish but have everlasting life" (John 3:16 NKJV).

From that Easter night in 1959 until today, I have been able to sing with unblemished confidence: "He lives, He lives."[2]

If you have not accepted this Savior today, I encourage you to invite Him into your heart. He came that you may have life and have it more abundantly. He came and died on the cross that you may have a right to live with Him forever in His kingdom. He wants to be your closest Friend.

Romans 10:9 (NIV) tells us how to let Him into our lives: "That if you confess with your mouth, 'Jesus is Lord,' and believe in your heart that God raised him from the dead, you will be saved." Confession and genuine belief are the criteria for salvation.

I've never seen Jesus in person. But on that platform that night, He became as real to me as any human being I've met. When I asked other people about the artist's rendering and how they felt that night, it seemed I was the only one who saw the actual blood flow from the body of Jesus. That was His way of confirming Himself to me.

When you are His and He is yours, He will confirm Himself to you in your heart in a way you can always remember. It may not be at the moment you invite Him in; it could be years later. But you will know by the Holy Spirit working in your life that you are accepted into the household of faith.

PRAYER

Thank You, heavenly Father, for loving us so much that You sent Your only Son to die on a cross so that we might be saved. You could have destroyed humankind with the tip of Your finger, but You didn't. Instead, You have chosen to live in our hearts so intensely that every day we are overwhelmed by Your love. How exciting it is to know that one day we will see the Savior of the world face-to-face! That will be an indescribable day of jubilee. Amen.

GOD'S WORD TO YOU

There is salvation in no one else; for there is no other name under heaven that has been given among men, by which we must be saved. (Acts 4:12 NASB)

AFFIRMATION

I am saved by the blood of the Lamb of God who has taken away the sins of the world.

The Call Up Yonder

God Promises
Eternal Life

My mama had two strikes against her all her life: she had a paralyzed right arm and foot. For the last six years of her life she was ill, and poor circulation was a challenge. Eventually she was confined to bed because she was nearly immobile. However, her mind was alert. She enjoyed dressing up every day, applying her makeup, donning flashy earrings. People stopped by her apartment daily to tease her and enjoy her teasing them.

In 1996 Mama's body began to deteriorate rapidly, and she had to enter the hospital. During her long stay, my sister and I experienced the pain and joy of seeing our mother prepare for death as we, too, attempted to prepare for the inevitable. Her body was broken down with abrasions. Her feet and legs suffered from sluggish circulation. She was unable to eat comfortably because of an apparent stroke. She couldn't move her body from her neck down without assistance. Yet she never lost her sense of humor. She never forgot how to sing the songs of the church. She never forgot how to pray. She never stopped watching or listening to Christian television. She did not forget to celebrate her birthday.

The doctors would tell my sister and me that they marveled at the high pain tolerance Mama had. She never complained. But then, I'd never heard my mother complain about anything. She'd always say, "I hope so!" She never lost hope that things would improve.

Her tolerance of pain, lack of appetite, sore body, failing circulation, and long, quiet hours were signs that she was about ready to meet her Maker. Sometimes I spent the night in her hospital room in the vacant bed next to her. I watched her for months, knowing in my heart that it would not be long before my sister and I would be motherless.

It really hit me one day as I watched her sleep. I wanted to ask her if she was ready to die, but I didn't know how. My daughter Lesa is so close to the Lord; I called her to ask her what I should do. "Just ask her!" Lesa said. "You know she's a Christian. Don't worry yourself! Find out how she's feeling about preparing to meet God."

I got up the nerve to ask her. "Mama, do you love the Lord?"

"YES!" she answered with gusto.

"Are you ready to go where He is?"

"NO!" she said emphatically.

When I told my sister about my exchange with Mama, we both interpreted her response as a sign that she might get well. She was always determined to get what she wanted! But within a few weeks her earthly determination turned to a holy longing for her heavenly home. We saw it in her eyes, her smile, her soft speech.

I began to pray that God would take her home. She had suffered enough. We told the medical staff there would be no more surgeries. We did everything we could to make her comfortable.

The Thursday before her death is something I will never forget. I stopped by the hospital on my way to choir rehearsal at my church. She was sitting up in bed, watching television, teasing the staff, talking to some of the patients who came by to see her, eating, and having a good time. I hadn't seen her so beautiful in years. Her hair was shiny; her cheeks were rosy; her nails glistened with her favorite red polish. When I got to rehearsal, I reported that my mother was better that day than she had been in years. But I'd seen enough sickness to know the signs of death. I knew it wouldn't be long. I was right. Mama died three days later.

We honored Mama's life with a joyous home-going service. I read to the family these assurances about the death of a Christian:

1. The death of a Christian is not the end of life, but a new beginning; death is not to be feared because it is a translation into another life. It is a release from the troubles of this world.

2. The death of a Christian is precious in the sight of the Lord. It is a welcoming to a better place: our Father's house where there are many mansions and where we will receive a crown of righteousness. It is an entrance into peace and glory, into the presence of Christ.

3. The death of a Christian assures rest and security, fellowship with other believers, activities of worship and singing, the ability to identify family members and friends who have gone to heaven.

4. The consolation for Christians left in this world is that some day they, too, will be there to meet and greet their loved ones who have gone before.[1]

Death will always have its share of sorrow. We will always grieve when loved ones go on before us. But our grief can be less intense when we understand God's promises about eternal life with Him. All of us who love the Lord will experience a glorious transition when our mortal hearts stop beating. No wonder Mama liked to hear me sing to her during her last days: "Some glad morning when this life is o'er, I'll fly away."[2]

Hallelujah!

PRAYER

Dear Lord, sometimes death is harsh and bitter, and I grieve the deaths of my loved ones. But I draw blessed peace from the fact that those who know and love You live on. Death is not the end for those who die in the Lord. Thank You for Your Word, a source of great hope and comfort that calms my fears of death and gives me sweet hope for an eternal future. I can rest assured that when I leave this world, I will be safe in my Father's house. Amen.

GOD'S WORD TO YOU

When the perishable has been clothed with the imperishable, and the mortal with immortality, then the saying that is written will come true: "Death has been swallowed up in victory."

"Where, O death, is your victory?

Where, O death, is your sting?"

The sting of death is sin, and the power of sin is the law. But thanks be to God! He gives us the victory through our Lord Jesus Christ. (1 Cor. 15:54–57 NIV)

AFFIRMATION

I can rejoice in death because Jesus has overcome it and given me eternal life with the Father.

Praying All the Time

God Promises to Fellowship with Us

I love to pray. I guess I'd better since I spend most of my time doing it. I wake up in the morning praying. I pray in the tub; I pray while I wash clothes or water the grass; I pray when I'm talking on the phone or hugging my children or driving or exercising; I pray in meetings and during business negotiations; I pray on airplanes; I pray for the sick and the suffering and for people I don't know. You get the picture. In almost every situation, my mouth isn't moving, but my brain is grooving. In my mind, I pray all the time.

One day as I was hugging my son good-bye after a visit, he said to me, "You're praying for me again, aren't you?" I looked a bit startled because I hadn't *said* a word. I nodded my head yes. He said, "You're always praying. I can tell. You've done that since we were little. We all know it. But that's good, Mama. That's good. Thank you. Keep it up; don't stop now."

At other times, one of my children will call and ask, "Whatcha doin', praying?" My husband may walk into a room where I am and see me sitting very still, gazing into space. When I hear him attempt to leave, I'll ask him what he wants. "Just wondering what you're doin'," he'll often say. "Were you praying?" Most of the time I am. I tend to pray when there's no apparent reason to pray. I just love to fellowship with my heavenly Father.

Some of my prayers sound like this:

- "Lord, have mercy."
- "Help me, Lord."
- "Thank You, Jesus."
- "Speak to my heart, Lord."
- "Lord, are You listening?"
- "Lord, You know what I need; do it, please."
- "Help my children, Lord."
- "Put a hedge of protection around my family, Lord."
- "Guide my tongue, Sir."
- "God, why are You so slow?"

- "What's this all about, Jesus?"
- "Do You hear me, Lord?"
- "Am I supposed to keep asking You to do this, Sir?"
- "Look, Lord, I need an answer!"
- "Praise the name of Jesus."
- "I love You, Lord."

Some of those prayers may sound as if I'm a little sassy with God or disrespectful of Him, but the truth is, God is my Father and yours. He knows all about us. We can come boldly to Him, and He will understand exactly what we mean and the attitude with which we mean it. In other words, we can come clean with God. I don't know how your prayers sound, but I'm glad God can read our minds and know our hearts. When we realize that prayer is simply expressing the heart's sincere desire to God, in silence or aloud, prayer can become as natural as breathing.

When I'm in an attitude of prayer all the time, it's pretty hard to worry or to think of negative or evil things. People have asked me why I'm so happy all the time. I may not always be so *happy*, but I have the joy, joy, joy, joy down in my heart! Such joy can come only in the presence of the Lord. It's a joy that brings contentment when things are topsy-turvy. It's a joy that calms my fears and smooths my feathers and gives me peace when trials and tribulations are on the rampage. That joy surpasses all understanding as I trust in my Friend and Companion, Jesus.

Have you prayed today? Wherever you are and whatever you're doing, right now is a good time. You don't have to use any theological or flowery words. Just be yourself; He'll understand exactly what you mean.

If you don't talk to Him every day, why not start now and make it a habit to talk to Him whenever you think about it? That must have been how I started: just communicating with Him silently whenever He came to my mind. I think that's what Paul, Silas, and Timothy meant when they urged the Thessalonians to "pray without ceasing" (1 Thess. 5:17 NKJV). Praying continually involves abiding in the Father's presence, whether formal prayers are uttered or not.

God created us to have fellowship with Him. When you make a habit of talking to Him often, you'll make Him happy, and He'll make you content. There is joy in the presence of the Lord.

PRAYER

I am so glad You are always available, Lord. I can talk to You any time of day, anywhere I am, about any and every thing. I don't have to hold back anything from You. I can even cry, yell, or scream, or I can laugh, giggle, and have fun with You. Thank You for accepting all my methods of getting in touch with You. It's good to know that whatever style I use, You're eternally ahead of me. You already know what I feel and need, and You've already solved the problem, answered the question, or handled the situation before I ask. What a consolation! Thank You for being so in touch with me. Amen.

GOD'S WORD TO YOU

Evening, morning and noon
   I cry out in distress,
      and he hears my voice. (Ps. 55:17 NIV)

AFFIRMATION

I pray without ceasing because God wants
to hear from me.

If Two
of You
Agree

God Promises
to Honor
Our Prayers

⸎

Something nasty was in the air on October 29, 1996. Three people called me in a row to report that either they were going into the hospital for breast cancer surgery or a loved one was. First, Marsha called to tell me she was scheduled for surgery on her breast that day. We prayed together that the surgery would not be necessary, that God would perform surgery on her and heal her. I felt confident that our prayer would continue through my anointed friend Debra, who was going to be with Marsha. I have never in my life seen such unwavering faith as Debra has.

The next call came from my friend Peggy, whose daughter was scheduled for surgery that day. Peggy was distraught because she could not be there with Charlene and she had lost another daughter to cancer not many years before. Peggy and I prayed together that the Lord would watch over Charlene and that surgery would not be necessary. We also prayed that Charlene would not be upset that her mother could not be there with her. We prayed that she would have complete and total healing and that God would be merciful and spare her life.

My other friend, Shirley, called later that morning to report that she was in the hospital getting prepped for surgery as we spoke. Shirley and I prayed that surgery would not be necessary, but if she went through with it, there would be no complications and her suspected cancer would be benign and easily removed.

While waiting through the day to hear reports from my friends, I stood firm on God's Word: "Again, I tell you that if two of you on earth agree about anything you ask for, it will be done for you by my Father in heaven. For where two or three come together in my name, there am I with them" (Matt. 18:19 NIV). Jesus taught that there is great authority in corporate prayer. Where two or three who are committed to Christ pray in faith, He is in their midst. His presence imparts faith, strength, direction, peace, confidence, and grace. And He promises that when His children agree together according to His will, He will do what they ask.

At 2:30 that afternoon, Marsha phoned. I heard glee, joy, and excitement in her voice. She was back home from the hospital six hours after she'd checked in. The doctors had examined her breast in preparation for surgery, and guess what! They found nothing. Another doctor was sent in to confirm the original team's findings. The medical professionals didn't know what happened, but they know what they saw on the original and subsequent X rays. Whatever it was had vanished. Hallelujah! No surgery necessary. Marsha was released and told to see a doctor in six months.

Two more hours passed before I heard from Charlene, my friend Peggy's daughter. Again, good news. Charlene was also back home—no surgery necessary. Her doctor told her to go home until he could figure out what was happening. Apparently her condition didn't appear to be as serious as he'd thought. Again God had moved in a mysterious way.

Several days passed and I didn't hear from my friend Shirley. On the following Sunday morning, I called Shirley's home to talk with her husband. She answered the telephone. She sounded out of it. But when she explained what had happened, there was again cause for rejoicing. Her tumor had been benign and was removed with no complications. However, the medication her doctor prescribed for pain was too strong or she did not need it at all. The day before I called, she'd decided to discontinue the medication. What I heard in her voice was only the sluggishness caused from several days of being overmedicated.

God demonstrated His miracle-working power in all three of my friends' lives. Marsha still has no symptoms of cancer. Charlene has not needed breast surgery to this day. Shirley has completely recovered. These cases are extraordinary to me, but not to God.

Of course, God works in His own mysterious ways and does not always answer prayers so promptly. I have agreed and prayed with people and have waited days and months to see the manifestation of God's power through answered prayer. But while I've waited, I've experienced the peace and contentment of knowing He will answer in His time. Sometimes I tease Him and say it would be nice if He showed up early every now and then! But His timing is perfect. Healing my three friends during that short period of time was a part of God's master plan for their lives.

When you pray with other Christians, believing in faith, and God doesn't show up when you think He should, don't get discouraged. Many times I have prayed believing that my prayer was part of God's perfect will, yet He didn't move as quickly as I wanted Him to. One time I had to wait sixteen years for Him to answer. But when He did, it was the right answer at the right time. While I was waiting on Him, I wondered what was happening. Sometimes I asked if He really heard me. Was I praying right? What else could I do? But deep within He assured me that He would see me through. He'll do the same for you.

PRAYER

Father, standing together in Your midst is the most confident place to be. Thank You for loving Your children enough to show us the manifestation of Your goodness through answered prayer. As You honor my prayers, help me to honor and trust Your perfect, mysterious ways. Amen.

GOD'S WORD TO YOU

Now this is the confidence that we have in Him, that if we ask anything according to His will, He hears us. And if we know that He hears us, whatever we ask, we know that we have the petitions that we have asked of Him. (1 John 5:14–15 NKJV)

AFFIRMATION

When I pray with other Christians according to God's will, I know our prayers will be answered.

The Answer Book

God Promises
to Reward Our Study
of the Word

*W*hen I was a little girl, my teachers at church would tell us that everything we wanted to know about was in the Bible. They told us the strange stories about Jonah being inside the whale; water parting and bunches of people walking through on dry land; Jesus feeding thousands of folks with a little bit of bread and fish; old man Noah building a huge boat and taking two of every kind of animal on it before the big rain. I was fascinated by the stories. But it wasn't until I became a teenager that I was forced by Mr. Beckett, my Sunday school teacher, to *read* the Bible because it really did give the answers to all the questions I had.

Still, my *love* for studying the Bible didn't come until after I married and started having major challenges in my life. I studied passages that dealt with what was going on at the moment—subjects such as forgiveness, work relationships, giving, family situations—and discovered that God's Word is as relevant today as it was thousands of years ago when it was written. And once biblical principles came alive in my mind and heart, I started practicing them, and they became a lifestyle. Now I can never get enough of reading the Bible. I want to be like the people in the synagogue in Berea: "Now these were more noble-minded than those in Thessalonica, for they received the word with great eagerness, examining the Scriptures daily, to see whether these things were so" (Acts 17:11 NASB).

Studying the Scriptures is critical for any believer who wants to grow in knowledge and wisdom. In Hebrews 4:12–13 (NASB) we're told, "For the word of God is living and active and sharper than any two-edged sword, and piercing as far as the division of soul and spirit, of both joints and marrow, and able to judge the thoughts and intentions of the heart. And there is no creature hidden from His sight, but all things are open and laid bare to the eyes of Him with whom we have to do." It is enlightening to know that the Bible has reflective power that gives us the ability to see ourselves as God sees us (Rom. 3:23). And when we see ourselves as sinners, we are told how to become clean and be received as members of the household of faith (Ps. 51:2; Eph. 5:26). Our guide for all of life is the Bible: "When thou goest, it shall lead thee; when thou sleepest, it shall keep thee; and when thou awakest, it shall talk with thee. For the commandment is a lamp; and the law is light; and reproofs of instruction are the way of life" (Prov. 6:22–23 KJV).

Do you have questions lurking in the back of your mind? Questions you don't want to ask anybody, or questions you've asked but haven't gotten satisfactory answers to? Let me recommend prayerful study of the Bible. When you pray and ask for clarity before you study, you'll be amazed at how God reveals to you just what you need at that particular time. He knows what you need before you do!

If you are not a regular Bible reader, I invite you to catch the excitement with me and thousands of others. Start a little at a time. Or think of a topic you want to know more about, and start with that. I guarantee you'll get enthused by what you'll learn, and someone will have to pry you away from your reading so that you can go to bed. There's no better book in the world than the Word of God.

PRAYER

Dear God, You gave brilliant men the ability to translate Your inspired Word so that people throughout the world can read, study, and understand. Thank You for making Your Word so relevant to my life today. And thank You for the gift of Your clear communication with all people; we don't have to second-guess You. Help me to remember that the rewards of knowing Your Word are great. Amen.

GOD'S WORD TO YOU

The law of the LORD is perfect,
  reviving the soul.
The statutes of the LORD are trustworthy,
  making wise the simple.
The precepts of the LORD are right,
  giving joy to the heart.
The commands of the LORD are radiant,
  giving light to the eyes.
The fear of the LORD is pure,
  enduring forever.
The ordinances of the LORD are sure
  and altogether righteous.

GOD WILL MAKE A WAY

They are more precious than gold,
   than much pure gold;
they are sweeter than honey,
   than honey from the comb.
By them is your servant warned;
   in keeping them there is great reward.
   (Ps. 19:7–11 NIV)

—————— ⚘ ——————

AFFIRMATION

As a faithful student of the Bible, I am rewarded
with growing knowledge, wisdom, and character.

You Shall Not Lie

God Promises Loving Discipline

*I*f there was one thing Granny hated more than anything, it was being lied to. When I lied, I made her the maddest. I could never figure out how she knew, but she could always tell when I was lying. She told me she had eyes in the back of her head, and I believed it! She told me she could look through muddy water and see the bottom, and I believed that too. Somehow, she always knew what was going on. Now that I have children, I have a better understanding of her intuition.

I'll never forget the time in kindergarten when I stole a dime. Well, I didn't consider it stealing; it was lying there, and I just picked it up. When I got home with a dime she knew I didn't leave home with, Granny asked me where I got it. I told her I found it. She interrogated me about where I found it, if I'd told the teacher I found it, how long I'd had it, why I didn't tell her about it, and on and on. Her interrogation seemed to continue for at least a lifetime.

Granny had a *way* about her when she thought someone was lying. She'd do the silent treatment thing until the truth came out. After I said I found the dime, she just looked at me strangely all evening, holding her thin brown lips tightly together—as if she loosened them, she might accidentally let a word slip out.

The next morning she was up bright and early, and I woke to her standing over me as I lay in bed. She looked like a giant. Her eyes were wide and questioning. She parted those thin, tight lips, and with a soft, but frightening voice asked me again, "Where did you get that dime? Don't you lie to me. If it's one thing I can't stand, it's a liar!" I was in real trouble now! I knew I had to face the music eventually, so I said, "I took it off the table at school." To which she replied, "Get up. Put your clothes on. I'm going to school with you this morning. You will stand up before the class and tell them you stole a dime and you are sorry. You will apologize to your teacher and tell her you will never do that again. And when you come home, I'm going to whip you for lying. If you had told me the truth, you might have been punished once. But now you'll get two punishments: one for stealing, one for lying. Girl, don't you know that if you'll lie, you'll steal, and if you'll steal, you'll kill? I will not have a lying, thieving killer in my house! You will not lie to me and live! I love you too much to see you grow up to be a liar. It hurts me to have to do this to you, but you will learn not to lie. Do you hear me? Do you understand, Girl?"

Yes, ma'am, I sure do. By the time she finished fussing with me, I wished she'd kept those tight lips tight.

The day went just as she planned. We got to school where she ushered me directly to my teacher, and I told her what I had done. Granny insisted that I needed to make a statement in front of the class. With tears of humiliation streaming down my face I said to my peers, "I'm sorry I stole a dime yesterday. I won't do it again." I don't remember how my classmates reacted; I just remember promising myself I would never be in that situation again!

When I got home that afternoon, there was Granny sitting in her favorite spot in the corner of that ugly brown velveteen couch. In her hand was a switch with three limbs platted together from off the old nonbearing mulberry tree in the front yard. She told me to come on in. She was going to whip lying out of me that day.

You would think I'd learned the lesson of a lifetime from that incident, but apparently I didn't because I remember another time I got caught lying to Granny. I was about nine years old and had just been released from Children's Medical Center in Dallas. I had been in the hospital because I was too fat. Fat had surrounded my heart, causing some medical conditions that were correctable only by losing weight. Within ten days in the hospital the doctors had reduced me to a normal weight for a child my age. When I was released to go home, I had to remain on the diet for months until my metabolism became regulated and my eating habits changed for good.

Patty, the little girl who lived next door to us, was out playing in the yard one day shortly after I got home. Granny let me go over to play with her. While we were playing, Patty was eating a Hershey bar. It looked so good. I ate one bite. Surely that wouldn't harm me. I held the chocolate in my mouth without swallowing it for as long as I could. I didn't realize that chocolate residue pooled visibly in the corners of my mouth.

When I went back home, Granny asked me what I'd had to eat. "Nothing," I lied. She pointedly asked if I'd eaten any candy. "No," I said. "Then what's that in the corners of your mouth?" she queried. I replied innocently, "I don't know." We went on like that for a little while. Then Granny let loose. I got severely fussed at about lying again, and then she cut some switches from the mulberry tree. Need I say more? The whipping and scolding went on for hours, it seemed. I heard the same lecture about lying and stealing and killing. Granny got her point across. I finally learned that a person's word is her bond. If I wasn't honest, I couldn't be trusted.

The fact that one of the Ten Commandments is "Thou shalt not lie" means that lying is neither a necessity nor an option. We don't have to lie, and we have no excuse to lie. Granny did me a favor by lecturing me and punishing me when I lied to her. She instilled in me the principle that honesty is always the best policy. This principle has guided me throughout my career, with my family, in all my relationships. God's commands make sense. Telling the truth is sure a lot easier than having to cover my tracks or face the righteous anger of Granny!

PRAYER

Father, You never tell us to do anything You don't equip us to do. So when You told us not to lie, You gave us the ability to tell the truth always. Help me to remember that You are the truth and that being Your child means I have Your spiritual DNA. Your blood covers me and enables me to do Your will. Thank You for Your loving discipline that helps rid my life of all deceit. Amen.

GOD'S WORD TO YOU

My son, do not make light of the Lord's discipline,
and do not lose heart when he rebukes you,
because the Lord disciplines those he loves,
and he punishes everyone he accepts as a son.
(Heb. 12:5–6 NIV)

AFFIRMATION

I welcome God's discipline because I know it is evidence of His love for me.

No Lone Rangers

God Promises to Use Each of Us in a Unique Way

$\mathcal{B}$ack in 1976, Judy and I worked together on the Dallas Institute of Banking board of directors. I was a director; Judy was the administrator. Not being able to see the future, I had no idea that the Lord was planting a person in my life who would be a wonderful source of creativity for my speaking business many years later. In fact, I never thought of Judy as a creative person. We never had that kind of interaction.

A couple of years ago we were together in my office and began brainstorming about things that could bring money into the business and help finance my television program.

Watching and listening to Judy, I discovered a different person. The person I had known was the corporate executive building an organization from a meager beginning to a thriving operation. The person sitting in my office now was a sensitive wife, mother, and grandmother, a businesswoman, and a creative genius. Judy is an organizer, strategist, analyst, creator, and implementer of workable ideas—ideas that included creating a ministering postcard, greeting cards, pocket cards, T-shirts, and other products that would benefit people and honor God.

God has prepared everybody and everything we need to carry out His will for our lives. To each of us, He gives the particular talents He wants us to have, and He plants us in one another's paths to assist in accomplishing what He wants us to do. The fact that no man or woman is an island is evident when we look around at all the people who help us succeed. I can't count the people who have been instrumental in my success. I could never do it all on my own! Nor does God want me to.

I can't help thinking about the time I was determined to play the piano. I *knew* that God would allow me to learn to play like my talented friend, Dr. Shirley Gregory Harris. Piano lessons were drudgery. I struggled and struggled with those lessons, sat at my piano for hours trying to make music come out of it. No music ever came. Noise did! I even bought a new piano, thinking that something was wrong with the first one. But nothing was wrong with the piano; something was wrong with the pianist! I had absolutely no aptitude to play an instrument of any kind. The sad thing about me and my piano struggle is that even though I loved my friend Shirley, I did not like the idea that she could play and I could not. I envied her.

Finally, after three years of torturing myself with the constant practice of imperfection, the lightbulb came on. I thought, *Silly girl, God did not give you the gift of piano playing. He gave you the gift of singing and speaking. He gave Dr. Shirley Gregory Harris the blessed gift of playing the piano. Get that through your thick head! Shirley can't sing; you can. You can't play; Shirley can. Wouldn't it be logical to ask her to play for you when you sing? God has given all of us gifts to magnify Him with. Why are you cutting off your blessing by envying someone's God-given gift? Get a grip!*

So I went to the telephone and called Shirley. I asked her, "The next time I sing, will you play for me?" Shirley replied, "Thelma Lou, I've been waiting on you to ask. Sure, I will. The Lord bless you, Child!" Ever since that day more than twenty years ago, Shirley and I have presented music together, and we are an anointed, dynamic duo. God has given us the gift of praise and exhortation through music. Isn't He amazing?

The Bible tells us that each of us is given gifts of the Holy Spirit. First Corinthians 12:7–11 spells them out:

> *Now to each one the manifestation of the Spirit is given for the common good. To one there is given through the Spirit the message of wisdom, to another the message of knowledge by means of the same Spirit, to another faith by the same Spirit, to another gifts of healing by that one Spirit, to another miraculous powers, to another prophecy, to another distinguishing between spirits, to another speaking in different kinds of tongues, and to still another the interpretation of tongues. All these are the work of one and the same Spirit, and he gives them to each one, just as he determines. (NIV)*

And Ephesians 4:11–13 (NIV) instructs us, "It was he who gave some to be apostles, some to be prophets, some to be evangelists, and some to be pastors and teachers, to prepare God's people for works of service, so that the body of Christ may be built up until we all reach unity in the faith and in the knowledge of the Son of God and become mature, attaining the whole measure of the fullness of Christ."

God uses all of us to accomplish His purposes. He established His body in such a way that no one person has all it takes to fulfill every ministry and mission on this earth. God's children must work as a team.

God knew before I was born what He had for me to do and who would help me. At every juncture, He supplies the people, places, products, and all the pieces I need to help me carry out His plans. Judy is one of those powerful pieces. Moses had his brother, sister, father-in-law, and tribal leaders who helped him manage the children of Israel. Paul had Barnabas and Timothy to help keep the churches together. Jesus had His disciples whom He left to carry the good news. He also had His inner circle of brethren whom He depended on to assist in His great camp meetings. Even God Almighty in Jesus Christ didn't try to be a Lone Ranger.

It's encouraging to consider the people who have helped you become the person you are. Those who are in your corner pushing and encouraging you all the way. Those who have different interests, skills, abilities, and expertise from what you possess. I am amazed to see how God gives every person attributes that are distinct from everyone else's. There are billions of people all over the world, yet God makes them all different. Incomprehensible! Our uniqueness is so satisfying when we are willing to use every person's special gifts to the glory of God.

PRAYER

Father, You demonstrated Your creative powers when You put order to a world that was without form. And when You created humankind, You made sure that no two people are alike. That blows my mind! Lord, thank You for providing everything we need when we need it to help us accomplish the tasks You have assigned us. Remind me not to be a Lone Ranger, but to celebrate and use every person's gifts in my efforts to further Your kingdom. Amen.

GOD'S WORD TO YOU

Just as each of us has one body with many members, and these members do not all have the same function, so in Christ we who are many form one body, and each member belongs to all the others. (Rom. 12:4–5 NIV)

AFFIRMATION

As a member of the body of Christ, I have a unique role to fulfill—and so does everyone else.

Ode to
Mrs. Taylor

God Promises
the Fruit
of the Spirit

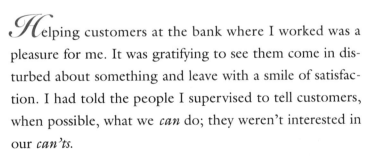

*H*elping customers at the bank where I worked was a pleasure for me. It was gratifying to see them come in disturbed about something and leave with a smile of satisfaction. I had told the people I supervised to tell customers, when possible, what we *can* do; they weren't interested in our *can'ts*.

Early one Monday morning, Mrs. Taylor came into the department ranting and raving, as mad as a wet hen. She demanded that the women do something they could not do. They were professional and explained what her options were, but she didn't like the options!

Several times they tried to reason with Mrs. Taylor, to no avail. I had trained them to get me if they couldn't solve a problem or handle a person. They got me.

I approached Mrs. Taylor and calmly attempted to explain what we could do to help her. It was not good enough. I have never seen anyone so irate. She kept yelling at the top of her lungs. She was so angry that she cussed me for everything she could think of. While I was being royally cussed, I kept eye contact and maintained a look of sincere understanding on my countenance. I let her vent!

When she finished, I explained that I understood how she could be so upset about her situation. However . . . and then I repeated what I'd already told her. (That's called the Broken Record Method.) Mrs. Taylor became even more irate and started gesturing with her hands, fingers, elbows, fists, and other auspicious parts of her anatomy while adding new cuss words to her tirade. All the time she was ranting and raving, people who thought they wanted something out of their safe-deposit boxes decided they didn't need anything. They stopped to watch the action. People who were en route to the break room decided they didn't need a break. They stopped to see the show. A lot of people were entertained that morning by the dramatic expressions of Mrs. Taylor.

She finally headed toward the elevator and left without being helped. I went back to my office content that we had done all we could to assist her. I was satisfied that I exercised self-control in handling that explosive situation. A gentleman who observed most of the action asked me, "Madam, how could you stand there and take that from that woman? I would have pulled her over the counter." My response to him was, "Sir, I was doing everything I could to help her. I was not going to go down to her level. I'm not any of 'those people' she called me. I know who I am!"

Six years later (not months, but years), I was teaching a course at the American National Bank in Austin, Texas. Guess who was there? Yep, Mrs. Taylor. She came to me during the break and asked me if I knew who she was. Honestly I had forgotten how she looked. I did, however, recognize the name on her name tag. She explained to me what had happened that long-ago day like this: "The day I was in the bank, my husband and I had lost everything we had. We've moved to a small town near Austin to start all over again. I'm now a teller in a bank." That was her way of vindicating herself, of saying she was sorry. We had a brief, but friendly talk.

Can you imagine how Mrs. Taylor must have felt when she thought about how she acted that day? She was not a bad or nasty person; she was a frightened, embarrassed, humiliated person feeling out of control. As I look back to that day, I'm so glad God gave me the choice of losing my cool or maintaining control. I chose to be empathetic and compassionate and not retaliate when Mrs. Taylor was calling me names. I could have justified getting upset with her and reciprocating her attitude, especially when she talked ugly about my mother. But I didn't. Thank God, I didn't. You see, I have never lost a business, home, car, and everything I own. I don't know how I'd act if that were to happen to me. I can say only how I hope I'd act. I've lived long enough to never say never.

Flying off the handle with people is not the response Jesus would use. As Christians, we are expected to bear the fruit of the Holy Spirit. When we accept Christ as our personal Savior, the Holy Spirit dwells in us and manifests His fruit in our lives. One fruit is self-control. When Mrs. Taylor was disrespecting me, something within me kept me from getting angry at her. I never felt the desire to be mean to her. All I wanted to do was help her.

Another fruit of the Spirit is love. The only way we can fulfill the will of God in our lives is to be love-inspired, love-mastered, and love-driven. A person controlled by the Holy Spirit needs no law to cause her to live a righteous life. I imagine we've all been in situations where self-control was difficult to maintain, but we will bear the fruit of God's Spirit if we surrender to Him.

PRAYER

What a joy it is to be controlled by the Holy Spirit! Because the Spirit is aware of all things, He will guide me into all truth. That includes showing me how to respond to others in love, especially those who are doing or saying unkind things to me. Lord, I trust You to manifest Your spiritual fruit in me in every situation. Amen.

GOD'S WORD TO YOU

The fruit of the Spirit is love, joy, peace, patience, kindness, goodness, faithfulness, gentleness, self-control; against such things there is no law. Now those who belong to Christ Jesus have crucified the flesh with its passions and desires. (Gal. 5:22–24 NASB)

AFFIRMATION

The fruit of the Spirit grows in me because
I belong to Christ.

Go Ye

God Promises
to Be with Us
When We Witness for Him

$\mathscr{A}$ lot of times I find myself dodging my responsibility to witness to people who may not know Jesus. You know, the package boy in the grocery store. The taxi driver who picks me up in unfamiliar cities. The hotel receptionist. The business client. The acquaintance in the beauty shop. The attendant at the service station.

But for Christians, the charge we're given is not optional, and it comes with a promise: "Go ye therefore, and teach all nations, baptizing them in the name of the Father, and of the Son, and of the Holy Ghost: Teaching them to observe all things whatsoever I have commanded you: and, lo, I am with you alway, even unto the end of the world" (Matt. 28:19–20 KJV).

This security from God is promised to us when we witness, winning the lost to Christ and teaching them to obey His righteous standards. It's comforting to know that whether we are weak, strong, reluctant, forceful, shy, assertive, covert, overt, bound, or free in presenting Christ to people, He never leaves us by ourselves. Jesus is alive and present in each of His children in the person of the Holy Spirit. He emboldens us to share the gospel message.

The good news of the gospel is that Jesus Christ was born, was crucified, and rose again that we may have eternal life with Him. God gave His only Son to die on a cruel cross so that we may be saved from our sin.

People in the Old Testament days who recognized God as Creator and sovereign Lord and accepted His authority as their Master were saved. Faithful people like Jeremiah, Joel, Abraham, Isaac, and Jacob are going to be in heaven with us. All the Old Testament writers were saved under the dispensation of the Law. But after Christ came, the Law became alive in Him because He came to fulfill the Law. After He died on Calvary's cross and rose on that third day, conquering death and hell, a new dispensation called grace was ushered in. Now we can tell the truly good news that the kingdom of heaven has come on earth in the form of a man to wash away sin in those who will receive Him. The Bible assures us, "For God so loved the world that He gave

His only begotten Son, that whoever believes in Him should not perish but have everlasting life" (John 3:16 NKJV).

Scripture spells out three specific requirements for salvation under grace:

1. Confession that we are sinners. We must recognize that our sinful condition separates us from God.
2. Belief that Jesus is the Christ, sent by God to die for our sins.
3. Faith that God raised Jesus from the dead to reign forever as Lord of our lives and King of the universe.

Salvation is the first step in becoming a practicing Christian. After that, just like a baby, a person has to be nurtured and trained toward maturity.

Sometimes this salvation business becomes confusing because people have so many different opinions. Some believe that a person has to stop doing any kind of wrong before she can receive salvation. Others think they can do enough good works, such as helping people and being kind, to earn salvation. Still others think that because they were raised in a religious home, they are automatically saved. But Scripture clearly teaches that salvation is a personal relationship with God granted only to those who sincerely ask Christ into their hearts and believe by faith what the Scriptures say about Him.

The New Testament has more than forty Scriptures about effective witnessing. I suppose the two things that make Christians most reluctant to witness are the fear of rejection and the uncertainty of what to say and how to say it. I use a variety of methods to be a more effective soul winner:[1]

- Passing out or mailing a copy of my personally designed postcard, which carries a simple message of my love for Christ.
- Passing out pocket cards with a message of hope on them.
- Simply asking people if they are saved and explaining what I mean to those who don't have a clue.
- Guiding people in making decisions by giving them biblical principles and Scriptures to read.
- Answering my mail and including the plan of salvation and/or other encouraging passages of Scripture.
- Giving complimentary books, bookmarks, or other gifts that point to Jesus.
- Inviting people to a Christian play or outing.
- Wearing a Christian T-shirt or other articles of clothing or jewelry.
- Carrying and reading my Bible in public.
- Singing gospel music.

- Reciting Scriptures or Christian principles in my seminars or in general conversation.
- Treating people with a servant's heart of love. *They will know we are Christians by our love.*

I have discovered that God can use the simplest action, motivated by love, to fulfill His Great Commission through us. Perhaps the clearest evidence of salvation is living the kind of lifestyle Jesus would live if He were here today. One of the best statements about Christianity I've heard was made by a female evangelist I greatly respect: "Christianity is not a religion like most people think. Christianity is a life of imitating Jesus."

Ultimately God Himself draws people to His Son. He will perfect (complete) whatever we have begun. Our responsibility is to *go* in love and tell everyone within our reach about the Jesus we serve.

PRAYER

Lord, please forgive me when I am lax in sharing the good news about You. Please give me greater boldness to tell people about the salvation that can be theirs through faith in You. If I don't tell them, they may not hear it from anyone else. Thank You for promising to be with me when I witness for You and for helping me to imitate You in the world. Amen.

GOD'S WORD TO YOU

And He said to them, "Go into all the world and preach the gospel to every creature." (Mark 16:15 NKJV)

AFFIRMATION

I have confidence that God is with me when I talk to people about Him.

I'll Never Teach Sunday School!

God Promises
to Bless
Our Ministries

$\mathcal{R}$uby Rhone had just become general superintendent of the Sunday school program at our church and noticed that women between the ages of thirty-five and fifty-five were seldom attending. Her goal was to offer the opportunity to study God's Word to all age-groups in the church, but somehow that particular group had fallen by the wayside because there was no teacher. Ruby knew that many of us who were members of the church were in the choir and on the usher board. Why weren't we in Sunday school?

I had attended Sunday school throughout my childhood. Regular church and Sunday school attendance were a given in my family. When I grew up and married, I said I'd never go to Sunday school again. I'd had my fill! Let the children go because they needed Sunday school; I didn't. Anyway, it was too early on Sunday morning. I needed to rest because I had worked all week and needed some time to do what I wanted to do. That definitely did not include Sunday school.

Ruby called to nag me almost every week about teaching a new Sunday school class for women in the age-group that she thought was neglected. Ruby knew I was a speaker and quite influential with many of the women in that age bracket, which included most of my friends. Ruby had a dream, and I was one of the characters in it. Every time she asked me to please be the teacher, I told her, "No!" reasoning that Sunday morning was the only time I had to spend *quality time* with my husband. Her response was, "He needs to be in Sunday school too!"

How long can a person be refused? Until she gets the response she wants. Actually Ruby did not get the response she wanted. My response to her, after several months of her badgering, was that I would not be the teacher, but I would come to the class sometimes. At that point, she had gotten a commitment from five of us to attend the class and had gotten someone to consent to teach it. The six of us in attendance that next Sunday formed the Truth Seekers Class.

The lessons were eye-opening, the discussion stimulating, the fellowship fulfilling. Every person brought something into the class that seemed to make it whole. I started looking forward to Sunday mornings and the Truth Seekers Class. My obvious enthusiasm prompted Ruby Rhone to start nagging me again about becoming an assistant teacher. Finally I agreed. (I didn't admit I was a bit excited!)

Little did I know that Ruby had plans to promote the Truth Seekers teacher and give me full responsibility for teaching the class. I found that out in the next month's workers' conference for Sunday school workers. As the assistant teacher, I was the next in line to become the teacher. Ruby had won!

One of the best experiences I've had over the past fifteen years is being the teacher of that class. Members include science teachers, college professors and other educators, engineers, and medical professionals who challenge me to prove the truth of everything I teach. Corporate executives and employees and governmental workers add their business expertise. Childcare workers, homemakers, and volunteers express their nurturing tenets. Entrepreneurs who are sometimes control addicts love to try to take over the discussion. It's wonderful! I get to interact with all kinds of women, teach the

Bible, and be challenged, and I'm forced to *study* the lessons to avoid embarrassment when they ask me hard questions.

These years of teaching the Truth Seekers have been the most enlightening years of my life. I didn't realize when I accepted this responsibility that I would grow from it much more than the rest of the class. I didn't realize how much I did not know about the Word of God. I didn't realize just how much the affiliation with these women would enhance my life.

The original class of five has grown to fifty-five. We are close enough to one another that one cannot feel pain without the group feeling and coming to the aid of that pain. We have lent financial stability to the prison ministry that three of our members are active in each month. One of our members quit her teaching job to follow her calling as a foster mother. She and her family have lovingly cared for a number of children in their home. The Truth Seekers have been in prayer with her and her family during health crises and court cases and have witnessed the Lord's grace in healing a crack baby from the devastating effects of that condition. Many of us have lost parents and other loved ones during the past few years. We have comforted one another.

Some mothers have watched their children stray from their Christian upbringing and pursue drugs, alcohol, and crime. We have been there for these mothers, supporting and praying for them and theirs through the dark days. We've upheld those who are caring for their aged parents or relatives.

We've celebrated our birthdays, anniversaries, children's weddings, and births together. Many of us have traveled on vacations together. The most joyful time we have together is Sunday morning when we praise the Lord with songs and prayers before we enter into the study of the lesson. We are in one accord, praising God for His grace and mercy because He has brought us through the week and allowed us to assemble together again to edify one another and glorify Him.

Can you see what I would have missed if I had continued to refuse to be a Sunday school teacher? My life would be void of this kind of fellowship and these relationships. I discovered that teaching a Sunday school class was not just standing before a group and demonstrating one's ability to teach. To me, it is the ability to share wisdom from the Word while demonstrating compassion and care for women who need support and fellowship as much as I do. A high point of my week is being with the Truth Seekers.

God has given all of us a ministry, whether we know it yet or not. Some of us are gifted teachers; others may be nurturers, caregivers, peacemakers, writers, artists, singers, decorators, floral designers, musicians, and so forth. Whatever we get the most pleasure out of sharing with others can be a ministry tool in our hands. Whatever edifies human beings and glorifies God is blessed by God. What ministry does He want to bless in your life today?

PRAYER

Father, thank You for being patient with me. When You give me a ministry opportunity and I don't take it, just keep tugging at my heart. Please give me the desire to do what You have for me to do. Amen.

GOD'S WORD TO YOU

Each one should use whatever gift he has received to serve others, faithfully administering God's grace in its various forms. If anyone speaks, he should do it as one speaking the very words of God. If anyone serves, he should do it with the strength God provides, so that in all things God may be praised through Jesus Christ. To him be the glory and the power for ever and ever. Amen. (1 Peter 4:10–11 NIV)

AFFIRMATION

When I am open to God's will, He shows me how He wants to use me and blesses my work for Him.

Until He Was Seven

God Promises to Remove Our Guilt

A friend told me an interesting story about God removing our guilt.

Her husband, Jim, and she had no idea they were in for a tremendous shock—a shock that turned out to be a blessing.

She had noticed that her son, Tyrone, was spending a great deal of time and money on a little boy. He bought the child a bicycle for his birthday. He took the little boy riding with him.

Being a mother, my friend was proud of the time her son was taking with this little boy who, she thought, obviously didn't have a father. It was a noble and worthwhile cause. She didn't think twice about it.

Finally her son could bear to keep his secret no longer: he told his parents that from the time the child was three years old, they'd had a clandestine father-son relationship. Tyrone had attempted to be a part of the family, but the child's mother wouldn't allow it. "We were both teenagers when Brenda had our son," Tyrone explained. "When she told me about the pregnancy, I panicked. How would I tell my parents I was going to be a father? I reacted poorly and she took it personally. She decided that if I would not share in the responsibility of our baby, I could not, in any way, be a part of their lives. Even when I came to my senses and tried to apologize and make it up, she wouldn't have anything to do with me. It took her until three years after Troy's birth to allow me to come around to see him. I was crushed. I missed seeing my son. I wanted his mother for my wife. That was the most difficult time of my teenage life. I had come from a happy family where there were a mother and a father. I wanted the same thing for my child."

By the time Troy was ready to start elementary school, Tyrone had gotten so attached to his son that he didn't want to share him with anybody else. He felt he had missed his earlier years, and if other family members came into the picture, he would lose his place in line with Troy. But the older little Troy got, the more questions he asked. He wanted to know who he really was. Where had he come from? Who were his grandparents? Where were his other relatives?

Tyrone wondered, *How do you tell your mother and father they have a grandson? He's seven years old and already in school!* But he found the courage to tell them the truth, and a meeting was arranged for the family to meet his son. When Troy was introduced to the family, he knew all of them by name. Tyrone had shown him pictures of the family and told Troy a lot about them. It was love at first sight: he liked them and they loved him. My friend said, "I'll always remember that day. When Tyrone started to say, 'This is your aunt . . . ," Troy interrupted with "Sharon!" He did the same with his aunt Debra and with my friend. "And I know who this is," he said, looking at his grandfather. "This is Big Daddy Jim!" She looked at her husband, who was trying to keep back the tears. Big Daddy is what their children had affectionately called her husband's daddy, their own grandfather.

She immediately started a ritual of rubbing Troy's head and giving him a big hug, and it has continued through the years. The only problem is that he is now very tall and she's five feet tall. So she catches him around the waist, looks up at him, and asks, "How's the weather up there?" He always looks down at her with his boyish grin and big, bright eyes and says affectionately, "It's all right. How're you, Grand-mother? Love ya!"

They finally know the truth about their son's little friend. He is their grandchild. All they regret is that they were not a part of his life earlier. But God joined their families together in due season. And even though both parents, Tyrone and Brenda, are married to other people, their spouses are wonderfully accepting and cooperative in blending the families. Troy has two brothers from his mother and two sisters from his father. Their family is complete because they have the blessing of enjoying all of their grandchildren.

Troy is sixteen years old and has only two more years in public school. He says he wants to be a policeman. That's a good thing. Debra's husband is a policeman; his brother is a policeman; some of their friends are police people. Troy has a lot of role models and a lot of love.

Perhaps you've made a mistake that caused you or some-one else guilt and pain. Can you imagine the pain and guilt of keeping a secret the way Tyrone did for seven years? It's wonderful to know we don't have to live with silent, private guilt all our lives. There are people who will listen to us with under-standing. There are resources and agencies where people are trained to give us professional advice. And there are always God's mercy and His helping hand ready to lift us up out of guilt and shame and show us solutions to our problems.

Whatever may have happened in your past is over and should be done with. It's history. You can pack your guilt and shame away in a box, use duct tape around all the edges to seal it tightly, and put it in the trash where it belongs. It doesn't need to haunt you any longer. Why? Because Jesus cares about what happened in your past. And He cares even more about what you're doing today to recover from it. He wants you to bring it to Him, so He can fulfill His promise to you.

For them, God brought indescribable joy out of a teenager's moral mistake. He gave peace back to their son after seven long years of guilt and shame. And He gave them a precious grandson named Troy. God does not love them any more than He loves you. Take your burden to Jesus!

PRAYER

Father, thank You for the fact that I don't have to bear my guilt and shame all by myself. You are always there to give me wise counsel even when I don't trust someone else with my secrets. Thank You for providing ways and means for me to be cleansed of my guilt and go on with my life. Amen.

GOD'S WORD TO YOU

The LORD your God is gracious and merciful, and will not turn His face from you if you return to Him. (2 Chron. 30:9 NKJV)

———— ⚭ ————

AFFIRMATION

I trust God to remove all my guilt and shame.

Low Self-Esteem Is Not an Option

God Promises
Self-Worth
in Him

At one time or another, everybody experiences cycles of low self-esteem. Feelings of low self-worth can be brought about by conditional love, criticism, rejection, alienation, oppression, health problems, loss of a loved one, change, incompetence, threats, indecision, inadequate education, verbal or physical abuse, substance or alcohol misuse, religious oppression, social pressures, lack of organization, fear of failure or success, yielding to temptations, physical appearance, failures, regrets, poverty, phoniness, family and domestic challenges, financial dilemmas, back stabbing. Should I continue this list?

In my book *Bumblebees Fly Anyway,* I described what it feels like to have a serious bout with low self-esteem:

> A crisis of self-esteem cuts deep into the personality, slicing at every nerve that would try to tell you that you are valuable, worthwhile, and precious. It jabs and taunts with messages that say, "You'll never be anything. You'll never do anything significant. You're as necessary as dryer lint, and just about as attractive."[1]

Perhaps the things that cause your cycles of low self-esteem are not listed, but you know what they are. Or you think you do. But guess what? In my opinion, the greatest cause of low self-esteem is simply this: not knowing who we are in Christ. When we don't understand our origin and how essential we are to the universal scheme of God's plan for this world, doubts about our worth are the result.

Some signs of low self-esteem include the following:

- Grandiosity—the attempt to make people think everything we do or have is better than what everyone else does or has.

- Name-dropping—the attempt to make people think we are important by identifying the people with whom we have an association.
- Running away from obligations—being irresponsible.
- People pleasing—trying to please everybody all the time.
- Always apologizing—accepting blame for most things.
- Pessimism—constantly finding what's wrong in almost everything and everybody.
- Whining and complaining—often griping and playing the victim.
- Putting people down—gossiping maliciously.
- Oversensitivity—taking what people do and say personally when it may not be meant that way.
- Perfectionism—attempting to live up to impossible standards.

Many things can raise our self-esteem: unconditional love, being appreciated, laughter, friendly and wholesome surroundings, being paid attention to, being listened to, compliments, accomplishments, reaching realistic goals, accepting our appearance unconditionally, appropriate touch, deep family connections, successful social and community affiliations, financial stability, contentment with where we are in our lives, fulfilling and gratifying activities, taking time to relax and regroup, among others. Do we realize, however, that whatever we do to attempt to feel better about ourselves is superficial without the true foundation of self-esteem and self-worth? Unless we rely on God's perfect love for us and the Holy Spirit working in our lives, all our efforts and experiences are temporary.

Occasionally I still have pity parties, but they last no longer than an hour. I will not permit them to go on too long. Sometimes I have actually set my alarm clock to allow myself fifteen minutes of unbridled self-beating. The alarm reminds me that I've spent enough time raking myself over the coals and feeling down. When the situation seems really big, I might give myself up to an hour to feel bad. But that's plenty long enough. Part of me may want to stay in a defeatist mode, but my spiritual side reminds me: *Hey, Thelma, don't you know who you are? You are a King's kid! You can just take this situation to Him and ask Him to lift you up out of this state and restore your gladness. Don't you realize that nothing has happened to you that He doesn't know about? Don't you realize that He has already worked it out even before you asked? He loves you* perfectly *and completely. So get up, Girl! Pull yourself together. You are worth everything to God. That's why Jesus died for you, remember?*

I have found two other practical, simple things to do that help me feel better about myself when I'm doubting my self-worth: (1) talk kindly to myself, and (2) smile.

Many of our feelings of low self-esteem come from the way we talk to ourselves. When we tell ourselves we are worthless, ugly, clumsy, or sick; we can't do anything right; we can't learn; we can't do this or that; we look bad; or we are always a victim, we can't help feeling unworthy. Our thoughts control our words. Evidently we must be thinking these things if we're saying them to ourselves. We must consciously choose to change the words we say.

That's one reason I've included an affirmation at the end of each reading in this book. An affirmation is a positive word or phrase spoken in first-person singular, present tense, as if it has already occurred. The affirmation for this reading is: "I can always feel good about myself because of God's perfect love for me." This statement is not intended to be arrogant, haughty, or deceitful. Rather, it is an expression of the fact that we can love ourselves with the kind of love embodied in Jesus Christ. Because God has made us in His image and loved us so much that He would give up His only Son for us, it only makes sense that we should love ourselves God's way. God even told us to love our enemies *as we love ourselves*. Let's not get so pious that we miss the point.

There may be times when, for whatever reason, you don't love yourself. If you want to feel better about yourself and begin to repeat this affirmation, it can help. One of my favorite affirmations is: "I can do all things through Christ who strengthens me" (Phil. 4:13 NKJV). Sometimes when I repeat this affirmation, I am not doing all the things I can do. However, I am reassured by this Scripture that when I rely on the One who works through me to do all the things He wants me to do, I am whole and victorious.

Smiling is therapeutic as well. When I'm feeling sorry or sad, I remind myself to smile. I try to think of things that make me happy (such as my grandchildren!). Sometimes I read something funny, watch a comedy on television, or talk to somebody who makes me laugh. Smiling and laughing are good attitude adjusters. Our facial expressions tend to control how we feel about ourselves and others around us. People who smile as a lifestyle are less susceptible to anger, frustration, agitation, aggravation, and other "ations" that easily pull them down. People who seldom smile often feel angry, sad, and bad about themselves.

People with high self-esteem seem to do these things:

- Smile often.
- Seldom make excuses or run away from obligations.
- Look for the best in people.
- Take risks.
- Adapt well to change (are flexible).
- Seldom talk badly about people.
- Enjoy varied interests.

- Display an eagerness to learn new things.
- Keep an open mind.
- Accomplish excellence rather than pursue perfection.

So much of how we feel depends on how we choose to think. We can decide to dislike ourselves or to enjoy ourselves the way we are. We can decide to have a pity party or to cancel ours and refuse to go to someone else's. As Christians, we don't have the option of having low self-esteem. Jesus paid for all our sins and faults so that we wouldn't have to beat ourselves up for what we have experienced or done.

Next time you feel bad about yourself and begin to doubt your worth, follow King David's example by reciting the truth of who you are in God:

For you created my inmost being;
your knit me together in my mother's womb.
I praise you because I am fearfully and wonderfully
made;
your works are wonderful,
I know that full well.
My frame was not hidden from you
when I was made in the secret place.
When I was woven together in the depths of the earth,
your eyes saw my unformed body.

All the days ordained for me
were written in your book
before one of them came to be.
How precious to me are your thoughts, O God!
How vast is the sum of them!
Were I to count them,
they would outnumber the grains of sand.
When I awake,
I am still with you. (Ps. 139:13–18 NIV)

God already knows who you are, but you will feel better when you hear yourself telling Him. When you are aware of the value God places on you and of how perfectly He loves you (as only He can), low self-esteem will no longer be an option. Hallelujah!

GOD'S WORD TO YOU

There is no fear in love. But perfect love drives out fear, because fear has to do with punishment. The one who fears is not made perfect in love. (1 John 4:18 NIV)

AFFIRMATION

I can always feel good about myself because of God's perfect love for me.

R-E-S-P-E-C-T

God Promises
Consideration
for All People

$$\sim\!\!\!\infty\!\!\!\sim$$

The flight from Singapore to Perth, Australia, turned out to be a free seminar for the gentleman sitting in the seat next to me. I had just finished teaching a seminar in Singapore called Negotiating Skills for Secretaries of the '90s. It had been a challenging day because secretaries in Singapore were women who did not have the option of negotiating. They were expected to answer the telephone, take messages, and keep their desks organized. Learning how to negotiate was not high on their list of priorities. All day I'd had to rework the seminar as I went along so they could take something from it that they could actually use.

When I got on the airplane, I determined that I was going to interview someone who knew the Australian people

GOD WILL MAKE A WAY

91

regarding what is expected of secretaries so that I could avoid making the same blunders I made in Singapore. I like the aisle seat; it puts you at an advantage. If the person in the window seat gets annoyed with you, he or she has only one out: that's by you. Just being in the aisle seat gives you some control of your seat mate's activities.

I gathered from his briefcase and attire that the gentleman sitting next to me was a businessman. As he fastened his seat belt, I spoke to him and asked his name. He hesitated a moment before telling me, but I was pleased to detect an Australian accent. I told him my name, which he clearly didn't care to know. While he adjusted his legal-sized yellow pad and got into position to write, I interrupted him by asking, "What do you do?" In a tone that clearly communicated, "Leave me alone," he told me he was a district manager for some big concern in Australia. I knew then that he was my subject to interview.

I said, "Great, you're just the person I need to talk to!" He was not a happy camper. "I need to ask you some questions," I continued, and then I told him about my experience in Singapore.

"Do you have a secretary?" I asked.

"Yes," he replied.

"What do you expect from your secretary?"

"What? What do I expect from my secretary?"

"Yes."

After a few seconds in a "well, let me think about that" position, he answered, "I expect her to outthink me."

"Oh? That's wonderful! And do you empower her to out-think you?" I asked.

He looked at me with disgust and asked, "What in the world are you talking about? What do you mean, empower?"

I was glad he asked! I explained what *empowering* means:

- Giving people responsibility with accountability
- Giving them ownership of projects and ideas
- Allowing them to make decisions and supporting them in their decisions
- Keeping them aware of what's going on in the company overall
- Allowing them the freedom to do their job their way within established guidelines
- Being a mentor and teaching them everything you know
- Showing concern for their well-being
- Giving them appropriate feedback and expecting the same from them
- Showing appreciation for their work
- Praising them when appropriate
- Giving them credit for their ideas
- Assisting them in advancing their careers

The gentleman put his pen down, looked me in the eye, and said, "Look, lady, all this stuff about empowerment is a lot of bologna. People are hired to do a job. If they know what they're doing and get paid for it, you don't need to compliment them and praise them and help them all the time. If they can't do the job, they can get out. I'm not going to spend my time making people feel good. I want them to work!"

He didn't know it, but he was in for a seminar. He had planned to go back to that yellow pad, but I had other plans for the brother. I leaned toward him and asked him some other questions:

"Are you having much turnover in your company?"

"How's the morale of the people who work for you?"

"Are you experiencing a high volume of mistakes?"

"Are people taking all their paid sick days?"

"Do they work because they like working there or because they feel stuck there?"

"Can you honestly say you are happy with the way things are going around your office?"

The man laid his pen down more gently, got into a listening position, and let me talk. I explained to him that there are four basic personality styles. These personality styles are not right or wrong, good or bad; they are just the styles people tend to fall into during certain interactions in their lives.

Each style is driven by certain goals and needs and is characterized by distinct behaviors and mannerisms. When we understand these styles, we can better understand how to work with and respect other people while bringing out their best.

Briefly, I detailed these personality styles for him.

The Control Freak or Decision Maker: This person is *task oriented.* He needs to be in charge, have his way, make decisions, avoid small talk, and get to the point with people. Sometimes he can be alienating and manipulative, but he can be depended on to get the job done. But how do you deal with him effectively if you are different? Remain businesslike. Don't beat around the bush when you have to tell him something. Don't waste his time with trivia when there is work to be done. Respect the fact that he knows what he's talking about most of the time. If you need to confront him, be sure you know what you're talking about. Time is important to him, so don't barge into his office unannounced and expect him to be polite and tactful. Don't take what he says or does too personally. At least you won't ever have to second-guess how he feels. This type of person doesn't need a lot of compliments. He knows he's good.

The Helpful Honey or Peacemaker: This person is *relationship oriented.* She needs to feel wanted and appreciated. She is personable, kind, tender, committed, concerned, the glue that holds things together, and easily intimidated by the Control Freak. She is often passive or passive-aggressive, meaning she holds her feelings inside until they get so bottled up that they explode. She has a memory like an elephant and will never forget anything you've done to her or for her. She operates best on compliments, appreciation, and support. If she makes you a promise, she'll do her best to keep it. Often she'll overextend herself in an effort to please and support other people.

So how do you deal with her if you're different? Give her a little time to talk. Ask her personal questions about her life and her family. Give her your vocal approval of something she's done. Allow her the opportunity to set some priorities and make some decisions without criticism. She is capable of shouldering a lot of responsibility, but she may not solve a problem as quickly as the Control Freak will.

The Data Chip or Thinker: This person is *task oriented*, but in a different way from the Control Freak. She needs to make sure that what she's supporting with her efforts is viable. She is precise, organized, systematic, concise, and able to read between the lines. She can be unimaginative and resistant if she doesn't think a project can work. She may be described as the "no" person—the one who says no to most things until she's had an opportunity to analyze them, think about them, test them, and repeat the process several times.

If you have a deadline and are expecting her to help you achieve it, you'd better make her deadline much more liberal than yours.

How do you deal with a Data Chip person if you are different? Give her information in writing, not orally, and make sure your presentation is organized. When she gets it in writing, she can think through it and analyze it without much delay. Disarray throws her into a quandary. Ask her for her opinion on an issue or project. She's usually already figured out the mistakes and loopholes in it, but may not express what she knows until the project is under way or finished. Then she might say, "I knew all the time that it wasn't going to work, but nobody asked me."

The Attention Getter or Enthusiast: This person is *relationship oriented,* but differently from the Helpful Honey. He needs to be noticed and is the life of any party. He is warm, polite, charismatic, articulate, often flashy, and a bit show-offy. He may volunteer for a lot of things but do little in terms of actual work. He's a good pretender, though; he enjoys taking the credit for a job well done when he actually delegated the job to someone else. Like the Control Freak, the Attention Getter wants you to think he knows it all, but he is often only a superficial information gatherer.

So how do you deal with him effectively? Give him what he wants. Applaud him. Let him talk. Support his volunteerism but hold him accountable. Laugh at his jokes. Express your enthusiasm. The thing that really turns him off is a pessimistic person.

"Now, sir," I asked my seat partner, "which personality style do you exhibit most of the time?"

"I guess the first one," he said. "I don't need anybody wasting my time and beating around the bush. I can't stand to be around honey-dripping people. They irritate the heck out of me."

Our conversation had gotten serious. He was listening and agreeing with much of what I was saying. He admitted, "Maybe I've been a little too harsh. I never tell people when they're doing well. I never compliment people. I'm losing the best secretary I've ever had, and I think it's because I never let her know how great she's doing. I've been told before that this is not a good way to manage people, but I didn't really listen. Thank you for the information."

Then I hit him with the clincher: "What else did you learn from our conversation?" I felt comfortable asking because the chance of ever meeting him again was remote, and I didn't have a thing to lose. He calmly and gently said, "I've learned that people have their own way of acting and behaving, and everybody won't act like me or think like me. I must learn to respect other people's personality styles even if I don't like the way they do things. It's going to be hard for me to practice this, but it's worth a try. My turnover rate is deplorable, and I think it's because of me."

Our conversation that began on the runway in Singapore came to a close at the gate in Perth. What had started out as an interview had turned into a lecture about the importance of respecting people's different personality types. As I reflect on that interesting day, I think of how important it is for everybody to understand how to deal with people on *their* level. Much confusion and irritation in dealing with people would be minimized if we'd only meet people where they are and respect their unique approach to life and problem solving.

When the Bible talks about respect, it refers to having high regard for others. We are to observe and discern the truth about people, show compassion and understanding, and behave with consideration so that the good qualities and attributes in them can be brought to the surface. Consideration and respect cause people to blossom.

I was washing dishes one day while listening to Aretha Franklin sing her jivin' song "R-E-S-P-E-C-T." *That's exactly what people need from other people,* I thought. Employers need to respect their employees, and vice versa. Students need to respect their teachers and authority figures, and vice versa. Church members need to respect their ministers and religious leaders, and they need to be shown respect in return.

And Christians should always demonstrate respect for everyone everywhere. As believers, we are obligated to do the following:

R—Regard each person as highly as we regard ourselves.
E—Extend a helping hand whenever needed.
S—Serve one another in love as Jesus did.
P—Protect one another from danger.
E—Evangelize the world.
C—Commit to helping others be their best.
T—Turn distrust into trust.

God expects us to respect one another. A psalm asserts, "The LORD is gracious and full of compassion, / Slow to anger and great in mercy" (Ps. 145:8 NKJV). If God can have compassion (respect, regard) for us, we can surely have compassion and respect for other people.

Perhaps you're in charge of other people's activities at work, school, home, or play. Making an effort to discover what makes them act the way they do can decrease your stress and improve communication. It's actually fun to watch the interaction of different personality styles and see how they complement and balance one another. Every successful team needs a decision maker, a peacemaker, a thinker, and an enthusiast. God made all of us unique so that we can take up the slack and fill in the holes of life and circumstances with our distinct personality styles. Let's appreciate and respect one another as He does.

PRAYER

Father, You are so wise, You can't make a mistake. You have given all of us our individuality. No two people are alike. Please help us to be better observers of one another. Give us the compassion and respect we should have for one another's differences so we can encourage one another to be our best. Thank You for modeling what consideration for all human beings is about. Help us to imitate You. Amen.

GOD'S WORD TO YOU

Then Peter began to speak: "I now realize how true it is that God does not show favoritism but accepts men from every nation who fear him and do what is right." (Acts 10:34–35 NIV)

AFFIRMATION

I will respect other people the way I want to be respected—the way God respects us all.

A Marriage Made in Heaven

God Promises to Bless Marriages

On one of my trips from Athens, Georgia, to Atlanta, a woman introduced herself to me and told me she was on her way to get married for the third time. She said she was sure that her second husband had been the mate God had chosen for her, but that evidently He had something else in store for them because her husband had run around on her and she couldn't take it. She explained that he was a Christian, and both of them worked in their church's children's ministry. He was a good father to their sons, but he just couldn't leave the women alone. He had already married the last woman he'd left her for.

I thought a minute about what she'd said and responded, "No, ma'am, God did not have different plans for you that caused your divorce. God never works in opposition to His plan for lifetime faithfulness in marriage. But Satan has a plan for every good thing God made. Because God ordained marriage as the first institution, and it was good, Satan does all he can to destroy the sanctity and purity of marriage. Don't blame God for your divorce. Put the blame where it belongs: on the devil."

It is bewildering to me how people become so vulnerable that they allow the enemy to control them to the point of breaking their marriage vows. I also know, however, that there are weaknesses inside all of us that we must fight with the aid of the Holy Spirit. I would imagine that most married couples believe deep down that their marriage is forever. Most of them may believe they are married to the mate God has divinely prepared for them. And yet, many marriages are plagued with sexual infidelity, physical and psychological abuse, drug abuse and alcoholism, actual or emotional abandonment, and financial catastrophe. Whether these issues arise occasionally or frequently, they can take their toll on the union.

I truly believe that many marriages that have ended in divorce were marriages made in heaven. Satan, the enemy of God and God's children, is a liar, schemer, and deceiver, and he takes pleasure in destroying what God has joined together. If you know without a doubt that God put you and your spouse together, I encourage you to be diligent in prayer and fasting when troubles come. Jesus said to the disciples, "I tell you the truth, if you have faith as small as a mustard seed, you can say to this mountain, 'Move from here to there' and it will move. Nothing will be impossible for you" (Matt. 17:20 NIV). And He added that some things don't happen without "prayer and fasting" (Mark 9:29 NKJV). We need to persevere when we ask Him for help and healing.

My marriage has gone through tremendous trials and temptations. I married very young, the day after my twentieth birthday. I entered marriage with the fairy-tale idea ". . . and they lived happily ever after." Little things, such as not being able to go shopping together because George didn't like to window-shop, caused anger. I was frustrated that he left his shoes, socks, and underwear lying around and expected me to pick up after him. I didn't know that came with marriage! Larger things troubled me, too, such as when George made major financial decisions without my input. (He once sold my favorite car without talking to me about it. It didn't matter that the buyers were his parents; I was his wife!) Even though we were able to straighten that out and it never happened again, I thought more than once, *This marriage stuff ain't all it's cracked up to be! What happened to living happily ever after?*

More than twenty-five years ago, one situation got gigantic. George admitted to infidelity—the straw that broke the camel's back. I seriously considered divorce. But thanks be to God, the Lord sent help! We discovered that His grace is sufficient for *all* our needs, including putting a broken marriage back together. I will never forget the early-morning phone call we received one Saturday in 1974. On the other end of the line were C. L. Walker and his wife, Thelma.

"Are you up, Thelma?" Mr. Walker asked me.

"No, sir," I answered.

"Well, wake up and put George on the phone."

I obeyed.

"George and Thelma," Mr. Walker said, "I don't know what's going on in your house, but the Lord didn't let me sleep all night, praying for and thinking about y'all. Whatever's happening, it's not good. God is not pleased, and the two of you had better get it straight. My wife and I want to pray for you right now." Mr. and Mrs. Walker then prayed words of admonition to us and petition to God for our unity, decisions, peace, and problem solving. I couldn't believe somebody was praying for us! The Walkers knew nothing about our problems; we had confided in no one at the time.

There was no doubt in our minds that the Holy Spirit prompted the Walkers to call us.

After that prayer, my husband and I went back to bed, but neither of us could go back to sleep. We lay completely silent except for the intense breathing and intermittent sobbing I was doing. Suddenly my husband turned to me and said something I will never forget: "Thelma, Mr. Walker is right. I've done everything to you that I guess I could have, but you've always stayed a good wife. If you forgive me for what I've done and how I've hurt you, I promise I will never deliberately do anything to hurt you again. It's over with her. I'm done with this. There's nothing out there that I want more than you, and I'm not leaving my wife for anybody. I love you."

"I love you too," I told him. "But I hope you're being straight with me. I'll forgive you, but it'll take some time to forget. I want a whole husband, not a piece of a husband. If you can promise you will be that, I'll accept your apology."

Praise God, I can honestly say that from 1974 on, my husband has kept his word. He has been a whole husband. He has supported me in all my endeavors. He is my prayer partner and my greatest fan. We have gone through trials related to our finances, children, health, and so much more together since that time, but God made our marriage in heaven. He was faithful to keep His promise to us to bless our marriage in spite of us. That fateful day renewed our relationship with each other and solidified the marriage God had divinely orchestrated for us. Satan was playing his ugly hand in our marital affairs by creating battles of discord, unfaithfulness, bitterness, and anger. But God won all the skirmishes and ultimately won the war. Now we do not look back at what was; we appreciate what is, and we look forward to wonderful tomorrows.

Our marriage was saved by the prayers of a few Christian friends, my praying and fasting, my husband's desire to do right, and wise counsel from Granny. I knew deep down that God had joined us together permanently although I thought, at one point, I was ready to end the marriage. Thank God, I didn't. Now, every day, we happily celebrate more than thirty-six years of oneness.

It may not always turn out so well. Marriages do break, and some are not repaired. But God is always faithful to heal and restore broken lives. You can be sure that His love is greater than all your problems. Praise His holy name!

PRAYER

Father, thank You for bringing the institution of marriage into this world. The love that a husband and a wife can enjoy reflects (if only dimly) the love that Your Son has for His bride, the church. When You create a marriage in heaven, it is difficult for anything to kill it except the selfish intent of the partners. Help us remember that You have control over our marital affairs, and Your mighty power can solve whatever problems come along. Thank You for being a God of restoration. Amen.

GOD'S WORD TO YOU

But at the beginning of creation God "made them male and female." "For this reason a man will leave his father and mother and be united to his wife, and the two will become one flesh." So they are no longer two, but one. Therefore what God has joined together, let man not separate. (Mark 10:6–9 NIV)

AFFIRMATION

Because of God's grace, power, and blessing, my marriage can survive Satan's attacks.

GOD WILL MAKE A WAY

The Joys of Grandparenting

God Promises to Bless Our Descendants

❧

Have you ever seen the bumper sticker that reads, "If I had known having grandchildren was this good, I would have had them first!"? My husband and I can relate to that. We often get to be weekend "stabilizers" for our kids by taking care of our grandchildren. On many a Sunday afternoon, they descend on us with all their luggage and baby equipment. We love it!

If you are a grandparent, there is no greater legacy to leave your family for generations to come than your righteous love and faith. The apostle Paul encouraged Timothy by mentioning his bloodline of faith: "I have been reminded of your sincere faith, which first lived in your grandmother Lois and in your mother Eunice and, I am persuaded, now lives in you also" (2 Tim. 1:5 NIV).

Sweetness and tender compassion are wrapped up in a grandparent. Even when I have to caution or reprimand one of my grandchildren, I do it with an irrepressible gladness and a smile in my voice. I believe grandparents can play a powerful role by

- supporting the godly teachings of their children.
- setting a good example of what God expects from His disciples.
- showing no favoritism toward any of the grandchildren.
- encouraging the children as well as the grandchildren to seek the will of God in their decisions and choices in life.
- training the grandchildren to fear the Lord and turn away from evil.
- teaching the grandchildren to obey their parents, grandparents, teachers, and other authority figures.
- helping to protect the grandchildren from ungodly influences by being aware of Satan's attempts to destroy them.
- encouraging the children and grandchildren to attend a church where God's Word is proclaimed.
- teaching the grandchildren that God loves them and has a specific purpose for their lives.

- instructing the grandchildren in God's Word through conversation, family prayer, Scripture, Christian music, and family devotions.
- lifting up the children and grandchildren before the Lord in constant and earnest intercession.
- not interfering when their children are correcting their grandchildren.
- not giving the grandchildren everything they think they want.
- allowing the grandchildren to earn (by working) some of the luxuries they desire.
- exposing the grandchildren to some of the finer things in life, such as theater, opera, travel, fine dining.

The great thing about being a grandparent is that you don't have to do all of these things every day, just when you want to. My husband and I get to pamper our grandchildren, let them get away with no-harm-done antics, love them, and then leave them with their parents!

I'm thankful to God that we have lived long enough to see our children's children. If you have grandchildren, love them, train them, enjoy them! If you have grandparents, honor them and include them. God's heart is delighted by the loving interactions of the generations.

PRAYER

Dear God, You did such a marvelous thing when You established the family. The components of a father and mother, children, and grandparents are so orderly and well designed for the good of the family unit. Thank You for the unique role You've given to Christian grandparents. Let our lights so shine that our grandchildren will see our good works and trust and glorify You. Thank You for promising to bless our descendants in this generation and for generations to come. Amen.

GOD'S WORD TO YOU

He decreed statutes for Jacob

and established the law in Israel,

which he commanded our forefathers

to teach their children,

so the next generation would know them,

even the children yet to be born,

and they in turn would tell their children.

Then they would put their trust in God

and would not forget his deeds

but would keep his commands. (Ps. 78:5–7 NIV)

GOD WILL MAKE A WAY

---— ✺ —---

AFFIRMATION

God will bless my descendants when I am faithful to
teach them His ways.

A Cheerful Giver

God Promises to Reward Our Faithful Tithing

The apostle Paul told the Ephesian elders, "In everything I did, I showed you that by this kind of hard work we must help the weak, remembering the words the Lord Jesus himself said: 'It is more blessed to give than to receive'" (Acts 20:35 NIV). That's good theology. But how many of us find it extremely difficult to give when we are barely making ends meet? Or when we're living on a fixed income and trying to save a little for a rainy day? Perhaps we have a lot of money but are reluctant to help some people who seem to need help every time we turn around. We might wonder, *If I can make it, why can't they?*

Have you ever wondered why *you* are always in need? You're struggling all the time. And as soon as you get a little ahead and think your financial situation is smoothing out, something comes along to mess it up. The car breaks down. The plumbing leaks. The air-conditioning fails. You need to buy new equipment for your business. Something costs more than predicted. The bills are due and you don't have enough money to cover them. Well, the Bible has answers to all of these dilemmas. I have found that God's Word concerning giving is true. God promises to reward us with blessing and protection when we give without reservation.

In Malachi 3, God accused His people of "robbing" Him by withholding their full tithes and offerings. He invited them to "test" His faithfulness by giving generously, trusting that He would "throw open the floodgates of heaven and pour out so much blessing that you will not have room enough for it" (Mal. 3:10 NIV). In the next verse, He also promised to "prevent pests from devouring your crops." For us today, I think those words mean that when we give to God freely, He will block or reprove anything that threatens to consume our financial security. As we give to Him, we will have peace of mind and the ability to meet our financial obligations.

There have been a number of people whose commitment to tithing and giving to my church I've noticed for more than fifty years. The late Deacon George W. Gregory Sr. and his wife, Zenobia, were prime examples. Even though they had seven children to take care of, the annual report of contributions showed that Mr. Gregory tithed out of every penny he earned. He worked two and three jobs to take care of his family, yet he made time to spend with his wife and children in support of all their activities. When the children got old enough, he took them to work at his night job. That family owned their home and rental properties, owned a car (when a lot of people were still walking), always had nice clothes, and were involved in church and community activities. Every one of those seven children became a college graduate. Mrs. Gregory was a kindergarten teacher, but she did not work outside the home until her two youngest children were old enough to go to work with her. People wondered how Mr. Gregory could make all that possible. I truly believe that because of his obedience to God concerning his finances, God honored him with financial abundance. Mr. Gregory was a great model to me of what following God's plan for giving was all about.

Deacon W. Timothy Beckett was another example. Mr. Beckett was a professor and an administrator in the Dallas Independent School District for many years. His education and high position in the field of education, the church, and the community did not cloud his perspective of what God's plan is for our lives in the area of giving. His wife, Helen, and he were always traveling to far-off places just because they wanted to. Their two children were well educated. His son is a dentist. His daughter is a businesswoman. Mr. Beckett wears tailored clothes and has always driven one of the finest cars on the market. He never seems to have a financial problem. Mr. Beckett is a perpetual tither and gives generously to many people. I sincerely believe he can do these things because he handles his money God's way.

Mind you, I realize that people who are not tithers progress financially too. But I have experienced the supernatural power of God with respect to my finances when I have obeyed His principles.

Years ago I deliberately entered into an intense study on tithing to prove to myself that the Bible did not require it. I definitely wanted to give myself a reason not to tithe. What I found instead is that Scripture spells out three specific kinds of giving that God's people are to heed:

1. *The tithe that belongs to the Lord.* Malachi 3:10 (NKJV) commands, "Bring all the tithes into the storehouse, / That there may be food in My house." We are to give part of what we have in this life directly back to God. We dare not rob Him of what is His.

2. *The offering that is a freewill decision.* Second Corinthians 9:6–7 (NASB) explains, "Now this I say, he who sows

sparingly shall also reap sparingly; and he who sows bountifully shall also reap bountifully. Let each one do just as he
has purposed in his heart; not grudgingly or under com-
pulsion; for God loves a cheerful giver."

3. *The alms for the needy.* These are things like clothing,
shoes, furniture, food, and other tangibles that we give out
of love to help less-fortunate people. Deuteronomy 15:11
(NASB) commands, "For the poor will never cease to be in
the land; therefore I command you, saying, 'You shall freely
open your hand to your brother, to your needy and poor in
your land.'"

I discovered there was no scriptural way out of giving
God's way! So I started giving—cheerfully. I trusted Him,
proved Him, and tried Him, and He never disappointed me.

Sometimes I was plagued by fear, other times by greed.
The fear was that I would not have enough money to meet
my needs; the greed was that I wanted to keep the money I
had and get more and more. I'll never forget this experience: I had started making quite a bit of money, which
increased my tithe substantially. While I was soaking in the
bathtub one Sunday morning debating with myself whether
or not to give "all that money to the church," the thought
entered my mind, *How can I expect God to give me big things
when I am not a steward of the little things?* I regrouped right

then and erased that greedy thought from my mind. I gave cheerfully!

I remember another experience vividly. Several years ago I was asleep in a hotel where I was to speak the following morning. About 5:00 A.M. I was awakened with an urge to get up and send a certain minister an offering. I had prayed several days earlier and asked God which person He wanted me to give an offering to, but was this His answer? I wrestled not only with the time of day I got the revelation, but also with the amount. *Say what? Give that much? It's too early, God. Lemme go back to sleep and I'll see if I still have this urge when I wake up!* But I couldn't sleep. God was trying to answer my prayer, and I was being difficult.

When I realized what was happening, I started thanking God for His answer. The urge grew, but the joy was even greater. I wrote the check and asked the Lord to reveal the address where I was to send it. Then I turned on the television. Lo and behold, the preacher I felt led to send the offering to was on the television and the address was on the screen below his name. *Whoa! Was that God's confirmation or what?*

Back home, something else happened that really confirmed God's leading. My husband said to me, "Thelma, I wrote this name and address down. We need to send this man some money." It was the same man I had already written and mailed the check to! I told my husband about my early-morning urge, and he just smiled in agreement and gave me a satisfied nod. George and I had gotten the same revelation. We gave liberally and cheerfully in complete obedience to God. What joy!

A few days later, we received the news that we had a large check coming in the mail to reimburse us for money owed to us that we'd forgotten all about. Some time after receipt of that money this Scripture came back to me: "He who sows sparingly shall also reap sparingly; and he who sows bountifully shall also reap bountifully" (2 Cor. 9:6 NASB). God was true to His Word!

Are you holding back from giving cheerfully because of fear or greed? Try God's principles. See if He keeps His word. Experience has taught me that God is the provider of everything. Both jobs and financial resources are provisions. And God promises to "supply all [our] needs according to His riches in glory in Christ Jesus" (Phil. 4:19 NASB). With that kind of assurance I can be a cheerful giver. Praise the Lord!

PRAYER

Father, sometimes I get lax with my giving and following Your principles regarding my finances. I allow people, places, things, fear, greed, disobedience, and stubbornness to get in the way of my giving. Sometimes I rationalize that what I know I need to give is too much, or I make the excuse that the money is not used the way I think it should be. But when I remember the amounts of money I pay Uncle Sam, the times I buy things I don't really need, the things I buy for other people just because I want to, I have to admit that maybe my love for them is greater than my love for You. God forbid. You have proved to me over and over that You take care of all my needs. In return, I will honor You with my giving! Amen.

GOD'S WORD TO YOU

Let the LORD be magnified,

Who has pleasure in the prosperity of His servant.

(Ps. 35:27 NKJV)

AFFIRMATION

I give cheerfully from the heart because I serve a God who supplies all my needs.

Family
Get-Togethers

God Promises
Kinship
in His Family

Family is so important. It's a great thing to have family and want to be around loved ones. Almost every week we experience a blessing when our children come to our home with their families and friends. Vikki sometimes brings her friends. George and Tina bring our granddaughters Vanessa and Alyssa. Our grandson, Tony, comes sometimes. Lesa comes with her husband, Patrick, and our other granddaughter, Alaya. We look for any reason to get together: Mother's Day, Father's Day when the Wells family reunion takes place, Easter, Christmas, Super Bowl Sunday, and every Sunday I'm in Dallas. Graduations, baby christenings, birthdays, anniversaries, baby showers, bon voyages, and even funerals are times to celebrate with a gathering at our house. There's nothing necessarily unique or spectacular about our family get-togethers, but everything we do is done in love.

Your family may not consist of a spouse, children, grand-children, or any immediate relatives. Maybe you have extended family members, or you consider your friends to be your family members. Whoever they are, they play a significant role in your well-being because you are bonded to somebody. Everybody needs somebody. That's why I believe family is so significant in God's overall plan for our lives. The family was the central unit of Hebrew society, and the concept of the family was often extended to refer to tribes, to the kingdoms of Israel and Judah, and to the Israelites as a whole.

Those of us who have accepted Jesus Christ as our Savior are a part of the greatest family ever created. We belong to the family (household) of God. God is our Father; we are His children. He accepts us, protects us, directs us, comforts us, disciplines us, loves us, and cares for us better than any human being could ever hope to do.

Greater than our relationship with our personal families is our heavenly Father's relationship with us.

George and I have so much to talk about after our loved ones leave. We rehash what the babies did or said, what's happening to the "old" children. How nice their friends are.

And how much they ate. We have so much fun! It's a rushing feeling of excitement that's hard to explain unless you have the same feelings. But that rush is nothing compared to the holy excitement we can enjoy as members of the household of faith. Do you look forward to the day when God's entire family will get together with Him for eternity? Can you imagine the singing, shouting, and running all over God's heaven?

My sister gave me a plaque that hangs on my wall. The words are self-explanatory:

> *A happy family is but an earlier heaven.*
> *Remember that children bring us up instead of the other*
> *way around.*
> *Faith is love taking the form of aspiration.*
> *Celebrate the rituals, birthdays, and anniversaries in*
> *your life with vigor and enthusiasm.*
> *Only our individual faith in freedom can keep us free.*
> *Rejoice in your loved one's triumph.*
> *Say something uplifting to one who is hanging their head.*
> *Walk hand in hand with truth and your family will follow*
> *(Anonymous)*

Jesus Christ said, "I am the way and the truth and the life. No one comes to the Father except through me" (John 14:6 NIV). If you have accepted Jesus as your elder Brother and God as your heavenly Father, then we walk hand in hand in truth as members of God's family. We are kin to God!

This babbling about family may seem trite to you. But when you consider those whose families are decreasing by separation of one kind or another, and those who have no family, this connection is vital.

On the Mother's Day after the death of my mother, I had a brief glimpse of what it must feel like to be without an earthly family. For a moment, I choked up when I remembered I have no mother, grandmother, father, grandfather. All I have left of my family members are my husband, children, grandchildren, sister, niece, nephew, uncle, and four distant cousins. As I realized that for the first time, the loneliness lasted only a moment. But in that instant, I suddenly felt the pain of the void that must be experienced by people who are apart from their loved ones.

If you have not kept in touch with your family members, or if you are estranged from them, make every effort to contact them—and keep in contact with them. They are probably just as lonely for you as you are for them. Make the phone call or visit. Write that letter or send that card with the pictures in it. If you've been estranged, you might be the one God has assigned to bring the family back together. The tugging in your heart to revive the relationship is not to be ignored.

God never ignores His family members. In the household of God, we never have to worry about separation or abandonment. Our Father is always available for whatever we need.

PRAYER

Father, the first institution You established on earth was the family. Thank You for allowing it to bring us so much happiness. The greatest family established is Your household of faith—the place where all God's children can come and be at rest. The place where there are no favorites, no taking sides, no fear of abandonment. The place of comfort and peace. The place of tender, loving care. When we finally get home, it will be a continual celebration of worship and praise with You forever and ever. Amen.

GOD'S WORD TO YOU

So then you are no longer strangers and aliens, but you are fellow citizens with the saints, and are of God's household. (Eph. 2:19 NASB)

AFFIRMATION

As a child of God, I am a valued part of His family, and I have constant access to my Father through the Lord Jesus Christ.

Mama T's Girls

God Promises
That a Virtuous Woman
Will Be Praised

When Lesa was in elementary school, she gave me one of the sweetest, most humbling compliments a mother could ever receive. "Mama," she said, "you're a Proverbs 31 mother."

"A Proverbs 31 mother? What's that?" I asked.

"You know! A mother who tells us good things and does the good things the Bible talks about in Proverbs 31!" Lesa replied.

I was shocked. What a thing to tell your mother! I had to study Proverbs and see exactly what Lesa was talking about. When I read it then, it meant a lot to me because of the compliment my daughter had given me. But it wasn't until years later that I absorbed the real meaning and took inventory of myself to see if I was deserving of such a compliment.

Are you aware that Proverbs 31 lists twenty-three attributes of a godly wife and mother? This came to my attention when I was planning my first television program. Looking at a godly woman through the eyes of Lemuel's mother opened my eyes to her varied traits:

1. Perceptive
2. Entrepreneurial
3. Industrious
4. Competent
5. Cool, calm, and collected
6. Clever
7. Resourceful
8. Charitable
9. A clear thinker
10. A powerful negotiator
11. A good people manager
12. A warm and compassionate wife
13. A financial planner
14. A real estate agent
15. A manufacturer
16. An effective communicator
17. Fashion conscious
18. Supportive of her husband
19. Appropriately submissive
20. Proud of her family and accomplishments
21. Devoted to God
22. Good with her hands and her mind
23. Wise

When I examined all those attributes, I marveled at how God has made women so complete that we are able, by His grace, to live up to all those standards. Of course, sometimes we slip. We make mistakes. But even when we fall short of the ideal depicted in Proverbs, we learn how to correct our mistakes and move forward.

After asking God to help me demonstrate those godly attributes for several years, I got a chance to teach them to prospective wives and mothers. No, not with married women expecting children, but with teenagers who, in about five or six years, would probably follow in the footsteps of their elders and marry.

Some girls at my church were sitting in the sanctuary one Saturday, apparently discussing some questions about how to conduct themselves when they thought older people were being discourteous to them. As I walked by where they were sitting, they stopped me and told me they needed to talk to me.

One of them said, "We want to find out how we can get these old people out of our business."

Now that statement got my attention! When I was a teenager, nobody thought I had "business." I had known some of their parents as little children when I was a teenager myself. My reply to the girls was, "Yes, we sure do need to talk." I promised them I would talk to their youth group leaders or parents and schedule an appropriate time to meet with them. I did, and we settled on the next youth meeting at church as a good time to discuss their concerns.

As the time approached, I prayed for wisdom in handling the young ladies. I opened the meeting without knowing exactly how I was going to conduct it, but I did know that God had been informed about the importance of my giving wise counsel. With a prayer on my lips, an open mind, listening ears, and my Bible in my hand, I began to tackle the questions.

It seems that some of the older women in the church had rebuked the teenagers about the too-short hemlines of their dresses, the clothes they wore to church, their makeup, and the way they wore their hair. The girls' point was that if their parents didn't mind how they looked, why was anyone else concerned? They wanted to know what they could say to people when they talked critically about how they looked. That was their "business." What a relief! I could easily talk about that. I chatted about the biblical principle of respecting one's elders. My advice was for them to tell the people who criticized them, "Thank you for caring about me!" That's all they needed to say. A comment like that would show respect for the person criticizing them while keeping the girls from getting hostile or angry.

Talking to these girls is a piece of cake, I thought. But the conversation continued into more sensitive and weighty issues. Things were getting so deep that we did not have time to discuss some of their concerns in detail. I asked the girls when a good time to finish talking would be. "Tonight at your house," they said. *Say what? Tonight? My house? Oh, man! I'm not prepared for this!* But after careful consideration of their needs, I consented.

They arrived at my house at 6:30 P.M. Oh, how they needed to talk! The subjects covered the gamut of sex, drugs, abuse, religion, vices, school, teen pregnancy. You name it, we talked about it. The girls had brought their Bibles. That was one of the requirements for coming to my house: they had to be willing to get their answers from God's Word, not my opinion. They needed the *truth*.

When midnight rolled around, I finally had to ask them to call their parents to pick them up. The girls asked me what they could call me. They didn't like calling me Mrs. Wells, and they had heard some of the older college students call me Mama T. So Mama T I became for at least a dozen young ladies. What a humbling position! These girls had enough respect for me to confide in me and ask for my advice. Their parents trusted me enough to let me be alone with their daughters and give them wise counsel.

"My" girls still were not finished with their questions and comments. We had to set another date for them to come back to my house. Next time, they wanted to sleep over. I consented on one condition: within the next thirty-one days they would have to read the book of Proverbs in its entirety. That was one chapter per day. At the end of that time, they could come back to sleep over, and we would discuss what they'd learned from their reading. If the next generation of young ladies was going to learn how to be good wives and mothers, I figured that the best source of information was the Bible.

Nobody taught me how to be a wife and mother. I had never heard of premarital counseling when I got married. Nobody had ever told me about Proverbs 31 and that I could live up to those biblical expectations and still keep my sanity. Perhaps if I had known what being a wife and mother was all about, I would have been more prepared, and the shock of my responsibilities wouldn't have been so overwhelming.

Several weeks after I got married and started doing some of the things listed in Proverbs, I also started resenting the fact that I had to do them. I thought it was all a great imposition on me, and I finally expressed my disillusionment and disappointment to Granny. She sat me down and told me everything I was expected to do. I didn't realize at the time that she was giving me a biblical description of a virtuous woman. It sounded to me as if I had been handed a life sentence to work hard, make my man happy at any cost, drive a hard bargain when I wanted to buy something, wash, iron, cook, sew, clean, pick up behind somebody, ad infinitum. All that did not suit my fancy! But as I matured and learned more about what God expected of me, I realized that Proverbs 31 is not suggesting that a woman do all these things without the help and support of others. The chapter clearly describes how a good husband respects his wife and how her children call her blessed.

Older women should be setting an example for younger women so when girls become wives and mothers, they will not be as disillusioned and disappointed with life as some of us were. One of the characteristics of the woman in Proverbs is her wisdom: "She speaks with wisdom, / and faithful instruction is on her tongue" (Prov. 31:26 NIV). After my teenage friends had completed their assignment of reading Proverbs, they asked me when I was going to keep my end of the bargain. We scheduled a date for our sleepover.

We had so much fun talking about their favorite passages. They were ready to have an intelligent discussion about some of the questions they'd been confused about before because they had started reading their Bibles with purpose. That night, I made them go to bed at midnight because we had to get up and go to Sunday school the following morning. It's really interesting having a group of teenage girls in your house when all of your own children have moved out long before! At least we had three bathrooms so they could use several dozen electric appliances without blowing our circuits.

That visit was not the last. They wanted to come back again. Their assignment before they could return was to read all of Matthew 6.

My relationship with these girls has continued in the most delightful way. I featured them on my television program because I believed the understanding they had gained of Proverbs 31 could help other young people and people in general. I was right. We got more requests for "the program with the girls" than for any other program I've done.

We never know who's watching us. We may not be aware of the example we set. It really doesn't matter whether we are married or single, have children or not. What matters is exhibiting godly attributes in our lives. Even though Proverbs 31 talks about wives, it makes clear that any woman who fears the Lord is to be emulated and praised. May we all strive to be women of noble character.

PRAYER

Master, You have given me the initiative, innovation, tenacity, energy, knowledge, and everything it takes to live a lifestyle that demonstrates the virtue that You, and You alone, can give. Thank You for the privilege of being a woman. Grant me opportunities to mentor younger women as they grow in virtue. Amen.

GOD'S WORD TO YOU

Charm is deceptive, and beauty is fleeting;
   but a woman who fears the LORD is to be praised.
Give her the reward she has earned,
   and let her works bring her praise at the city gate.
   (Prov. 31:30–31 NIV)

———— & ————

AFFIRMATION

Through desire, commitment, and prayer, I can
become a virtuous woman and earn the praise of
those I serve.

The Closet

God Promises
to Strengthen Us
When We're Persecuted

My mother was born with a paralyzed right arm and right foot. She was also a dark-skinned girl. My mother's mother, Mother Dot, was from black and white ancestry. She could have passed for white if she hadn't had kinky hair. A lot of African Americans in my grandmother's day thought "light is better" because of the attitudes left over from slavery. Dark-skinned blacks had worked in the fields and were given harder jobs, while light-skinned blacks had worked in homes and secured better jobs.

Some of my relatives told me that Mother Dot was not only ashamed of her daughter's skin color, but she also attempted to straighten out my mother's limbs by pulling, massaging, and twisting, to no avail. When she was unsuccessful, in her desperation she punished my mother by shutting her in a closet. My mother could never do anything to please Mother Dot.

My mother and I were forced out of the house when I was born, but my great-grandmother took me to raise when I was two years old. As I got older, Granny let me visit my other grandparents. Whenever my precious grandfather, Daddy Lawrence, was around, Mother Dot was fairly nice to me. But as soon as my grandfather left for work, that same closet my mother had been locked in became my place for the entire day. No water. No food.

Smell this closet with me. It reeked of tar and sweat from the old railroad boots my grandfather wore as a brakeman on a railroad train in Dallas. The wool clothes in the closet trapped body odor, and the mildew in the corners as well as the heavy-duty mothballs in the clothes made me sick to my stomach. That was one stinky closet!

But God is good. I had been around the church all my life and had learned many hymns by the time I was four or five years old. Just as children today learn television commercial jingles because they hear them so often, I learned songs of the church that had surrounded me. Inside the stinky closet, I sang songs like "What a Friend We Have in Jesus" and "Jesus Loves Me! This I Know." Those songs sustained me during my dark hours in the closet. As I sang, God gave me peace. I was not afraid. I even sang myself to sleep sometimes.

Today I have no sense of trauma. I have no malice against Mother Dot. God was with me during the abuse. At the time I didn't even know she was being abusive. Thank God, He keeps His word. He *will* strengthen us and comfort us when we are persecuted. Let's face it. There are things that happen to us in this world that we don't deserve, didn't want, and can't send back by Federal Express. But God is faithful.

As a little girl, I memorized the words of Psalm 27. What a comfort those words were during many dark hours!

> The LORD *is my light and my salvation—*
>   *whom shall I fear?*
> The LORD *is the stronghold of my life—*
>   *of whom shall I be afraid?*
> *When evil men advance against me*
>   *to devour my flesh,*
> *when my enemies and my foes attack me,*
>   *they will stumble and fall.*
> *Though an army besiege me,*
>   *my heart will not fear;*
> *though war break out against me,*
>   *even then will I be confident.*
>
> *One thing I ask of the* LORD,
>   *this is what I seek:*
> *that I may dwell in the house of the* LORD

all the days of my life,
to gaze upon the beauty of the LORD
    and to seek him in his temple.
For in the day of trouble
    he will keep me safe in his dwelling;
he will hide me in the shelter of his tabernacle
    and set me high upon a rock.
Then my head will be exalted
    above the enemies who surround me;
at his tabernacle will I sacrifice with shouts of joy;
    I will sing and make music to the LORD.

Hear my voice when I call, O LORD;
    be merciful to me and answer me.
My heart says of you, "Seek his face!"
    Your face, LORD, I will seek.
Do not hide your face from me,
    do not turn your servant away in anger;
    you have been my helper.
Do not reject me or forsake me,
    O God my Savior.
Though my father and mother forsake me,
    the LORD will receive me.
Teach me your way, O LORD;
    lead me in a straight path
    because of my oppressors.

Do not turn me over to the desire of my foes,
   for false witnesses rise up against me,
   breathing out violence.

I am still confident of this:
   I will see the goodness of the LORD
   in the land of the living.
Wait for the LORD;
   be strong and take heart
   and wait for the LORD. (NIV)

Whatever you've gone through or are going through, God wants you to know that He is with you and cares about your suffering. He wants you to call on Him and ask for wisdom on how to get out of abusive situations. Waiting on the Lord does not mean doing nothing while you wait for Him to come down and rescue you. It means doing what you know is necessary to get out of the situation while confidently anticipating God's help as you do it.

The Lord cares about you! When you're in the "stinky closets" of life, trust Him to put a song in your heart.

PRAYER

Father, I am so grateful I can depend on You to be with me during times when I am mistreated and can't see a way out. Thank You for giving me the inspiration and direction to make it through the pain and humiliation of abuse. Jesus, because You were a Man of Sorrows, acquainted with grief, You understand how it feels to be persecuted by the people who should have loved You. Help me to endure life's injustices with grace, and to escape from abusive situations with dignity. Amen.

GOD'S WORD TO YOU

For in the day of trouble
   he will keep me safe in his dwelling;
he will hide me in the shelter of his tabernacle
   and set me high upon a rock. (Ps. 27:5 NIV)

AFFIRMATION

A loving God will comfort and strengthen me when
I am hurt by this world.

A Ram
in the Bush

God Promises
That Jesus Is
Our Substitute

Hattie and I were supposed to room together at the 1997 National Speakers Association convention in Anaheim, California. I waited for hours for her to arrive at the hotel. No Hattie. The entire night passed before I heard a word from her. About 6:15 the following morning, Hattie called me to explain that there had been a death in her family and she would not be coming. She sounded composed, so there was no need for alarm.

At a little after five that afternoon, I received a call from the driver in the lobby of the hotel. He was there to transport Hattie to her book signing in Long Beach. I didn't know anything to say except, "She's not here. She won't be here because of an emergency in her family. I don't know what to tell you." Panicked, the driver asked me to call his boss, the bookstore owner, and give her the news. I did. She was in a panic too. She told me that Hattie's book signing was announced over the radio and in the newspaper. People had already started coming into the store for the seminar on her book.

The boss asked, "Are you a speaker? Do you have books? Can you come and stand in for Hattie?" She did not accept any of my objections, such as nothing to wear for the occasion; too much on my plate; I hadn't read Hattie's book (an important point). None of those excuses satisfied her. So I consented to stand in for Hattie.

The driver and I climbed into his open-air Jeep and sped bumpily along the Los Angeles freeway toward the bookstore customers waiting in Long Beach. With anxious anticipation, the owner stood in the downstairs doorway holding her praying hands together, fearful that I may not be the representative she needed for the occasion, but knowing I was the best she could get.

As soon as I entered the bookstore and introduced myself to her, I asked to see one of Hattie's books. Hurriedly I read through the table of contents, glanced through a few paragraphs, and assured her that I was ready for something I certainly had not anticipated.

There were about thirty people patiently awaiting Hattie's entrance. A teenager read an appropriate poem for the subject of the evening's discussion and then introduced me as Hattie's substitute. Off I went with the presentation of Hattie's book, *Women Who Carry Their Men*. I was glad Hattie and I were such intimate friends because I was able to interject some experiences we had shared and make the audience feel that they were getting a taste of the "real Hattie."

God does not make mistakes. My time was divinely ordained. Hattie could not be there, but He sent me in her place. My testimony and advice were valued because I spoke from my experience of marital victory through many ups and downs and battle scars. I became the role model for the occasion, someone the women could look up to with hope.

Granny used to say, when things got hectic and she didn't know what to do, "God's got a ram in the bush." She meant that we don't have to worry or be stressed when we don't see a way to meet our need because God does see and has provided a solution. He never leaves us without a ram in the bush. Abraham can testify to that. Because of Abraham's obedience to willfully sacrifice his son, God faithfully provided a substitute (Gen. 22:13). I was Hattie's ram in the bush. My willingness to substitute for her was symbolic of the price I was willing to pay for a friend.

Jesus was our ram in the bush. He was willing to endure pain and punishment so that we may be delivered from our sicknesses and sin. There has never been a more perfect substitution. Isaiah 53:4–5 (NASB) describes the scene:

> Surely our griefs He Himself bore,
> And our sorrows He carried;
> Yet we ourselves esteemed Him stricken,
> Smitten of God, and afflicted.
> But He was pierced through for our transgressions,
> He was crushed for our iniquities;
> The chastening for our well-being fell upon Him,
> And by His scourging we are healed.

Jesus always shows up for His appointments. He does not need a substitute because He *is* our substitute. He doesn't need someone to beg Him to act on our behalf. That's why He came to earth. As our Great High Priest, He is seated at the right hand of God making intercession for us, still standing in. Knowing that should take away all our worries and anxieties. Why should we bear them? We have a Substitute!

PRAYER

Jesus, when I think about the tremendous price You paid for us when You willingly became our substitute on Calvary, my heart is full of sorrow and gratitude. How can I ever thank You? You have set me free to live in Your strength instead of mine. Although coming through for someone else can't compare to what You did when You stood in for me, Your sacrifice is an example to me. Help me to imitate You by being the kind of friend to others that You are to me. Amen.

GOD'S WORD TO YOU

He himself bore our sins in his body on the tree, so that we might die to sins and live for righteousness; by his wounds you have been healed. (1 Peter 2:24 NIV)

AFFIRMATION

It is easy to perform sacrificial acts when I realize the price Jesus paid to be my substitute.

Transforming Moments

God Promises
to Satisfy
Our Souls

*A*telephone call that I received on a Monday morning in June 1996 changed my career dramatically. Although I had spoken to groups throughout the United States and in several foreign countries, the majority of the groups were composed of secular businesspeople. I had spoken for Christian groups all my life within my relatively small world of Dallas and a few other cities, but that's as far as my overt Christian message went. That was about to change.

The woman who at that time was the executive director of the New Life Clinic's Women of Faith conferences asked me that morning for an appointment to discuss the possibility of my speaking for the conferences. I had never heard of Women of Faith, but I did know of the good reputation of the New Life Christian counseling clinics.

When the director came to my Dallas office, she explained that the Women of Faith conferences were the brainchild of Stephen Arterburn, the founder and chairman of the board of New Life Clinics. His idea was to bring large groups of women together to listen to speakers share how they live with joy along this journey of life. The current theme of the conferences was "The Joyful Journey," and women were coming by the thousands to laugh and share and hear about the grace of God.

The director told me that on the previous weekend she had gone into a bookstore and was led to my book *Bumblebees Fly Anyway: Defying the Odds at Work and Home*. She had become absorbed in the book and was certain that God had inspired her to read it and ask me to travel with the conference. She was frank when she told me I would be a first. They had little or no black participation. She thought I could lend a lot of credibility to the venues and, at the same time, influence women of color to become more involved.

Little did the director know that I'd been asking God to give me a forum where I could minister to more people at one time than I could in the corporate world, without having to camouflage what I say or present some stale formula for success that does not involve the Word of God. I was filled with joy at the opportunity to work in God's vineyard in a forum that had already started attracting women in droves. When she asked me about my availability for the months of August, September, and October 1996, my schedule was completely open for the specific dates of the conferences. To me, that in itself was a miracle, and confirmation that God wanted me to be involved.

To contemplate the way God works in our lives is truly amazing. He'd had that June day planned for me before the foundation of the world. Before I was formed in my mother's womb, God had planned my going out and my coming in. Praise God!

My first Women of Faith Joyful Journey conference was in Allentown, Pennsylvania. I had never been part of a Christian women's conference of that magnitude. There were approximately six thousand women in attendance, and during my forty-five-minute speech, they laughed and cried and applauded. It was a transforming time for me. I knew this was it! This was where God wanted me to be. This was the fulfillment of the desire He had put into my heart. He had allowed a passion to grow in me that would be satisfied in this moment.

When I got back to Dallas, the director called and told me just what I longed to hear. "Thelma," she said, "my original thought was to have you be a regular speaker at our 1998 conferences, but you were such a hit, we'd like you to join us for the rest of 1997 if your schedule will allow. I know how busy you are. You may not have all the dates available, but check your schedule and let us know. If you can join us, we'll have a contract in the mail to you this week."

I wish you could have been a fly on the wall watching me and listening to my heart pound with excitement. I wish you could have seen the tears of joy streaming down my round cheeks, making white salt lines down my face. I wanted to jump up and do a holy dance! God showed His perfect plan for my life again: all the dates the director wanted were open. God was transforming my life right before my eyes with an opportunity I'd had no idea existed.

As of this writing, I have participated in fifteen Joyful Journey conferences. The attendance has doubled, and the power of God is becoming more evident in the lives of the speakers as well as in the lives of the attendees. Stephen Arterburn reported to the speakers that at the 1997 Sacramento conference, ninety-nine women accepted Christ as their personal Savior and twelve thousand asked for more information. That's what these conferences are all about: winning souls for the kingdom and encouraging women to exhibit joy, one fruit of the Spirit. I know God has me right where He wants me to be at this time in my life. His Spirit is touching, healing, reviving, regenerating, reestablishing, and reconciling thousands of women to His way of responding to life's ups and downs—through an earthly vessel like me. To quote Bishop T. D. Jakes, pastor of the Potter's House in Dallas, in an interview about his overwhelmingly successful growth at the Potter's House in just one year: "It makes you look like you have a great strategy. But it's God who has a great strategy, and then you stumble onto it."[1]

Our God is a God of order. He has already determined the path each life is to take to bring glory to Him and satisfaction to our souls. Our job is to seek His wisdom and be open, flexible, and adaptable to His plans for us that may—and more than likely will—alter our lives dramatically.

PRAYER

Father God, how I thank You for the significant moments in which You transform my life according to Your will. Before the foundation of the world, You ordained what I was created to do. You know exactly what will satisfy my soul. It's good to know that the path I take in response to Your direction is paved and ready for travel. I never really know where You are taking me because You surprise me almost every day! But I know You are orderly, organized, and sovereign. Therefore, I can trust Your transforming moments and embrace Your will for my life. Amen.

GOD'S WORD TO YOU

The LORD will guide you continually,

And satisfy your soul in drought,

And strengthen your bones;

You shall be like a watered garden,

And like a spring of water,

whose waters do not fail. (Isa. 58:11 NKJV)

GOD WILL MAKE A WAY

AFFIRMATION

I trust God to guide me to the activities and
relationships that will satisfy my soul.

Notes

Oh, Blessed Savior

1. Frederick Whitfield, "Oh, How I Love Jesus."

2. Alfred H. Ackley, "He Lives."

The Call Up Yonder

1. *The Full Life Study Bible* (Deerfield, FL: Life Publishers International, 1992), 732.

2. Albert E. Brumley, "I'll Fly Away."

Go Ye

1. Postcards, pocket cards, T-shirts, bee jewelry, and music tapes may be purchased by calling Thelma Wells, A Woman of God Ministries, at 1-800-843-5622 or writing 2038 Cedarcrest Blvd., Dallas, TX 75203.

Low Self-Esteem Is Not an Option

1. Thelma Wells and Jan Winebrenner, *Bumblebees Fly Anyway* (Dubuque, IA: Kendall/Hunt Publishing Company, 1996), 76.

Tranforming Moments

1. *Dallas Morning News,* religion section, Saturday, July 5, 1997.

About the Author

Thelma L. Wells is a woman of many dimensions—an author, speaker, former host of her own television show, retreat sponsor, organizer, executive, wife, mother, grandmother, and active community and church volunteer. In the past four years she has authored two books, *Bumblebees Fly Anyway: Defying the Odds at Work and Home* and *Capture Your Audience Through Storytelling*.

Christian and secular groups often call on Thelma as a speaker and trainer. She has worked with corporations, associations, and educational and governmental institutions, sharing her insights with more than 1,000,000 people in every state in the United States and in numerous foreign countries. She is a regular speaker for the national Women of Faith conferences, sponsored several times a year by New Life Clinics. She is a dynamic speaker with spiritual depth who embodies her message, "In Christ, you can be the best of what you want to BEE!"

Thelma has been married to George for thirty-six years, and they have three children and three grandchildren. She lives in Dallas where she runs her business, Thelma Wells, A Woman of God Ministries.

Prayer with feet

With my Prayers I mix my labors and
Sometimes God is pleased to bless the results

George Washington Carver
Educator, Scientist

Prayer is recognizing + cultivating an awarene
of God